SERIOUS FUN

Ingenious Improvisations on
Money, Food, Waste, Water & Home

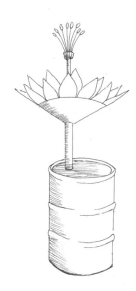

FINDHORN PRESS

DEDICATED TO
THE CREATORS OF THE WORLD,
WHO ARE ALL OF US.

SERIOUS FUN

Ingenious Improvisations on
Money, Food, Waste, Water & Home

CAROLYN NORTH

Line Drawings by Sharon Strong

FINDHORN PRESS

Published in 2010 by Findhorn Press, Scotland

ISBN 978-1-84409-540-7

Edited by Nicky Leach
Interior design by Damian Keenan
Front cover design by Sara Glaser, featuring the
"Raincatcher Sculpture" by Christina Bertea and Lauren Rollig,
at urban garden in late summer in Oakland, California.
Photograph by Meredith Stout.
Printed and bound in the USA

1 2 3 4 5 6 7 8 9 17 16 15 14 13 12 11

Published by
Findhorn Press
117-121 High Street,
Forres IV36 1AB,
Scotland, UK

t +44 (0)1309 690582
f +44 (0)131 777 2711
e info@findhornpress.com
www.findhornpress.com

CONTENTS

green press
INITIATIVE

Findhorn Press is committed to preserving ancient forests and natural resources. We elected to print this title on 30% post consumer recycled paper, processed chlorine free. As a result, for this printing, we have saved:

5 Trees (40' tall and 6-8" diameter)
2 Million BTUs of Total Energy
519 Pounds of Greenhouse Gases
2,499 Gallons of Wastewater
152 Pounds of Solid Waste

Findhorn Press made this paper choice because our printer, Thomson-Shore, Inc., is a member of Green Press Initiative, a nonprofit program dedicated to supporting authors, publishers, and suppliers in their efforts to reduce their use of fiber obtained from endangered forests.

For more information, visit www.greenpressinitiative.org

Environmental impact estimates were made using the Environmental Defense Paper Calculator. For more information visit: www.papercalculator.org.

MIX
Paper from
responsible sources
FSC® C013483
FSC
www.fsc.org

FOREWORD

For years we have been struggling to get across the message that big changes are coming and we'd better be prepared for them. Now the financial crisis, climate change, and even the way the planet itself is acting up—with earthquakes and volcanoes—and is bringing home the message that things are changing already. They are not the way they used to be, and they are likely to be less and less so. The term "sustainability," especially in its negative variant "unsustainability," has entered mainstream vocabulary. And so has the term "crisis."

What's the next step? It's exactly what Carolyn North's book calls for: Wake up, and don't just think but act!

The problem with such wake-up calls in the past is that people have been afraid to follow them. Acting means not just doing the same thing as always but doing something different. Or doing the same thing but differently. And that could be uncomfortable and entail a risk. Better stick with "tried and tested" ways of doing things.

Now all this could change. It could change by the simple expedient of reading this book. Because this is a textbook—destined to be a classic textbook—of doing things differently (and better) while also enjoying it. This is a new message, and its importance can hardly be overemphasized.

How wonderful to have fun and be good at the same time! Sounds implausible? Reading this book you'll find out that it's true. It's entirely possible. And on top of that, it's easy. Anybody can do it. So why not you?

These days the world of business offers the following insight: You can do good in the world *and* do well for yourself, too. The parallel insight waiting for you in this book is that you can do good in the world *and* have fun, too—fun doing good. There is no excuse anymore for not doing good. At least not doing the kind of good covered in this book—and this book covers a lot of territory. It covers almost everything you and I, and everybody else on this dangerously overexploited and maltreated planet, can readily do, both in the civil sphere and in our personal capacity.

I have been saying for a while that the two cardinal sins of our time are convenient complacency and facile skepticism. A bit of pertinent information can help us in deciding to get rid of both.

Complacency borne of the convenience of not having to change anything claims that things are basically all right as they are. There are problems in our world, and occasional crises, but they are being managed by those in charge—or perhaps they will just resolve themselves. The world has seen problems and crises before, and has muddled through without people like you and me doing anything about them. We don't need to bother trying to change the world—in the final count the world will take care of itself.

In the final count, convenient complacency is the sin of uninformed optimism.

Facile skepticism is the reverse of convenient complacency; it's the other side of the coin. It tells us that we don't need to change anything, not because things are basically all right as they are but because things cannot be changed—certainly, not by people like you and me. If we managed to get through problems and crises before, it may have been because we were just plain lucky, or because the problems and crises were not that serious. We cannot tell whether those problems and crises that lie ahead of us will be really different; they could be resolved by a happy turn of events, or could just play themselves out. In any case, there is not much we can do about it. The world is pretty much what it was in the past, and so is human nature. So, if we are still here tomorrow, it will not be because the world has changed, and certainly not because we have changed it. It will be because we are plain lucky, or because our problems are not that serious after all. And if our problems are really that serious, and we are not so lucky, then we won't be here. That will be too bad, but that's the just way it will be.

Facile skepticism is the sin of uninformed pessimism.

Why are do I say that these forms of optimism and pessimism are uninformed? Because they both ignore the most fundamental fact about our world: that it's no longer sustainable. It's on the threshold of chaos. If it doesn't change in time, it will collapse. But on the threshold of chaos, complex systems *can* change; and our world, at least in this respect, is an interacting and interdependent complex system. When such a system reaches the threshold of chaos, even small fluctuations can catalyze major changes. These are the famous "butterfly effects."

Doing good of the kind described in this book means being a "crucial butterfly." As Carolyn North will show you, it's not difficult, it's not painful, and it doesn't call for sacrifices. So why not do it? Go ahead, change the world, and enjoy it!

Of course, it's not quite as simple as that; but it is quite as important as that. It's certainly worth a try. So, forget being a complacent optimist or a facile skeptic: be a positive and fun-loving activist. You can't do better than that!

Ervin Laszlo, futurist philosopher
Tuscany, Italy
May 2010

INTRODUCTION

There are some things so serious, you have to laugh at them.
—*NIELS BOHR, PHYSICIST*

Be joyful although you know the facts.
—*WENDELL BERRY, POET*

On the Galapagos Islands, an archipelago of relatively recent volcanic islands in the remote ocean off the coast of Ecuador, an odd array of plant and animal wildlife has adapted cunningly to the harsh conditions of bare volcanic rock of the islands. The species that have managed to survive are those that have been ingenious about making use of the conditions in which they found themselves. There are cormorants with stunted wings who swim instead of fly; iguanas that feed on algae in the sea; huge, hulking tortoises foraging in extinct calderas; and finches whose beaks are shaped to take advantage of every kind of seed and insect in their environment. Even tomatoes have found a way of taking root in tiny cracks in the bare lava! As Darwin recognized, these islands are a laboratory for evolution.

It is also a known fact that among wolves, the pups with the lowest resting heartbeats are the ones who initiate play the best and these are the wolves who tend to be the leaders in the pack. Imagine: the relaxed rascal is the one identified as "wolf most likely to succeed!"

Being playful and adapting to new and possibly harsh conditions is how Nature evolves, and what this little book is about. It will look at how the natural world works and try to find the patterns by which Nature continually creates and sustains life, as it cycles, flows, balances, and forms networks of all its systems. As in the natural world, having to adapt in new ways to harsh conditions seems to spark creative new possibilities and unleash an unlimited array of responses we had no idea we had. We have life—is the product of a multitude of gifted people sharing with me their wisdom, their ideas and their company. Many of these friends are local and current; others are from everywhere and other times, but we are a community, and their wisdom is timeless and universal. The medium has been the message from the start and I have had a wonderful time playing and dreaming with them about how to survive beautifully in this crazy world of ours.

Old friends and new, we are improvisers together, and I bow to them with gratitude and friendship as we all try to find the most elegant path through the turmoil and angst of this time of tumultuous Worldshift. The world, whatever we do, shall inevitably evolve—with or without us. I'd like to be there if possible, surrounded by good friends and having a blast! Come join us!

The way I understand things, the deeper you go
into anything local, the more you find the global.
—YO-YO MA, CELLIST

CHAPTER ONE

MONEY

Work like you don't need the money;
dance like nobody's watching;
love like you've never been hurt.
—MARK TWAIN, HUMORIST

When I was 20 years old, I went to France on a French government scholarship to study art history at an institute of medieval studies in the small provincial town of Poitiers. Shortly after I arrived, I was given the unexpected opportunity to be a live-in nanny with a family, caring for the children in exchange for room and board. It was the perfect situation for me: a charming room in an attic that looked onto a cobble-stoned street, and around the corner a Romanesque church. I adored all five children, and the parents treated me as more of a guest than a nanny.

They also offered me an additional stipend for teaching English to the two oldest boys. I had more than I needed for the year and, deciding that my scholarship was superfluous, I offered it back to the institute so that some needier student than I could benefit from it.

Well! Such a kerfuffle that caused! The faculty had no idea what to do with me, and after many heated discussions behind closed doors, I was begged to please keep my scholarship. If I did not, I was told, the money would be sent back to the government to pay for bombs. Feeling very foolish, I had no choice but to accept as graciously as I could. So I went shopping. I had noticed a gorgeous quilted coat in the outdoor market with a fur-lined hood ...

I can laugh now, recalling the naive and idealistic girl I was then, but in fact I might be inclined to do the same thing today. Why not share my good fortune with others when I find myself with a surplus? That makes a lot more sense to me than runaway global capitalism, or a banking system so complicated nobody can understand it. And who can comprehend the fact that while some people are billionaires, others squat on our sidewalks begging for spare change?

Since I am totally baffled by what goes on in the economy, it is probably presumptuous of me to write about money. On the other hand, it may take just such an innocent—like the child who asked why the emperor wore no clothes—to ask a few deliberately naive questions, such as:

What is money, really?

What do banks do?

Does the money system serve us, and if not, who does it serve?

Are there creative alternatives to the money system?

What might they be?

Why, for example, it is that even as our economy is derived from what the natural world produces, and we humans take from it everything we need to survive, do we give so little back in exchange? That does not seem to make any sense. How can we not realize that without the natural world we wouldn't exist? Some obvious connection seems to have gone missing—the exchange part—and something self-evident seems to have gotten misconstrued—the value part.

The Ecology of the Economy

Braden R. Allenby[1], former research vice-president for Technology and Environment at AT&T, has observed the similarity of economics and ecosystems, in that each takes in materials and turns them into products. But, he points out, that while Nature's transformations are cyclic, our economies' transformations are linear.

In a natural ecosystem—a forest, for example—every plant and animal, weather system, and soil provides value for everything else in the forest. An ecosystem is a shared enterprise in which all organisms benefit, from the tiniest mite in the ground to the air, earth, and water around it. Nothing is wasted, and no organism consumes more than it needs.

Leaves and needles drop to the ground, providing humus that feeds the roots and fungal web in the earth, which maintain the lives of everything growing. Insects and animals are dependent on these plants and, in return, drop their poop and used-up skeletons to add to the soil in which the plants grow. The forest breathes *out* oxygen, which is breathed *in* by all creatures—including ourselves—and the web of tree roots filter the water that falls to Earth and feeds the streams that provide life for all of us.

It is a perfect feedback loop that keeps every part of the forest in dynamic balance and interdependent with every other part, growing and decaying and providing food and breath for one another. Any organism that grows out of its proper proportion with everything else destroys this balance, and disaster ensues. We know about this: in the human body we call it "cancer." Whyever would we imagine it to be good way to organize our economy?

I once saw a graphic example of where one-way consumption can lead, when a billygoat I knew got into the feed bin and ate a whole sack of grain. It fermented in his belly, which swelled alarmingly, and before we could help him his stomach had burst, and he keeled over and died.

The History of Money

So, the first question is: What is money, really? The dictionary defines money as: "a medium that can be exchanged for goods and services and is used as a measure of their value on the market."

Historians of money know that people were bartering as early as 9000 B.C., using livestock as a medium of exchange. In fact, the word "cattle" comes from a root word meaning "property." If I have a valuable pig, which you need, and you know how to make boots, which I need, I'll give you my pig and you make me a pair of boots, and we'll be even. Or, once people settled and grew crops, they exchanged produce: If I grow barley for you, and you grow rutabagas for me, we can make an even exchange and everyone benefits.

However, the person who has a pig does not always need boots, and the person who grows barley may not care for rutabagas, so tokens of value—some precious, scarce item to stand for the goods and services people needed—came into vogue. By 1200 B.C. in China, these were cowrie shells and metal spearheads and knives. Eventually, the metal tools were broken into bits and pieces, such as coins, which were used to represent the metal objects.

By 500 B.C., people were using precious metals—bronze and gold and silver pieces shaped, interestingly enough, like cowrie shells—as their medium of exchange; and by about 100 B.C. in China, squares of leather from the hides of white deer were what represented value. These were perhaps the first "banknotes."

I have heard tell that early in human history, in the area we now call Denmark, taxes were levied, and those who did not obey "paid through the nose," that is, they had their noses cut off! Ever wonder where that phrase came from?

Tribal and indigenous peoples practiced *potlatches*, or community gift-giving, as their way of distributing wealth. These served to bond people to each other as well as to provide the goods that everybody needed, and variations of the potlatch have been practiced all over the globe for millennia.

Hunting and gathering would take place during the warm months, and the goods would be stockpiled until a bounty had been procured. Then in the winter, great ceremonial feasts and giveaways would be held. The community would gather, feast, and celebrate with dancing and singing and theater. Everyone was expected to rival each other in generosity, to the benefit of all. It was barter on the grand scale, on the sacred scale, and played an essential role in the cohesion and mutual support of the members of a community.

In Polynesian society, the person chosen as "chief" was the one who was able to control and distribute surplus food, and among Trobriand Islanders, the exchange system was based upon "balanced reciprocity" in which certain items were ceremonially exchanged on a regular basis.

The gold standard was introduced in England in the 1800s, in which paper currency was backed by a storehouse of gold, and banknotes were printed to represent the amount of gold held in store. Rather than trade directly with this gold, people would be given pieces of paper that represented the gold, and they would exchange these paper bills with each other for the goods and services they needed. Their relationship with each other and with the storehouses of gold—banks—was based upon trust.

Now, even the paper certificates—the banknotes we carry in our wallets—have been replaced by credit cards, which are backed by little more than thin air and our belief that they are worth something.

Our second question, then, is: "Where does money come from?"

The answer, to my astonishment, is that money is simply printed out, like money for a Monopoly game. *Nothing* of value stands behind it. The idea that money has value is something we have all bought into, allowing our lives and our culture to be defined by it. Accepting this, we accept such notions as:

there is not enough to go around;

some of us will have it and some of us will not have it;

the poor will always be among us;

in order not to be one of those poor, we've got to compete with each other for what there is.

Lynne Twist,[2] founder of The Soul of Money Institute, calls this a mind-set of scarcity, in which we find ourselves afraid and competitive rather than trusting and cooperative with each other. The Keynesian economist John Kenneth Galbraith has put it bluntly, saying, "The process by which money is created is so simple that the mind is repelled."

How could it be that I did not know?

The History of Debt

Did you think that the Federal Reserve System was a governmental agency? I did. While the supervisory body, the Federal Reserve Board *is*, in fact, an independent federal government agency, the Federal Reserve System is a privately operated corporation owned since 1913 by 12 select top banks across the country that print out money—*our* money, to be exact—and lend it back to us with interest. How much money is printed out, and under what circumstances, is not entirely clear to me, but the effect is that some of us tend to get the short end of the stick. Often, the result is that we then have to borrow money to get by, having to pay interest on money that, as far as I can see, was our own to start with. Or am I missing something here?

Naturally, in order not to be among those left out, those who are clever at the game of accumulation take more than others. This cannot help but create a mind-set of scarcity in many people. It reminds me of the game of Musical Chairs, in which one chair—and one player—are removed after each round, causing everyone to try and grab one of the remaining seats when the music stops. Do you remember being nervous as you circled past those chairs?

I wasn't so surprised to learn, therefore, that the Koran has an injunction against the charging of interest. Jesus objected as well. And Shakespeare wrote a play about it. But we're still doing it, and that seems to be how bankers make their millions—on our debt. The way it works is that we owe the banks, with interest, more than they have lent us. It goes by many names and schemes that nobody (except perhaps the

Martín Prechtel,[6] the multigifted artist and author of *The Secrets of the Talking Jaguar,* suggests what he calls "love drive-bys." You leave a flower on someone's doorstep; you hand a stranger a poem. Then you move on. Or the woman living in a balconied high-rise who plucks leaves off her potted geranium plant and after writing inspirational words on them—HOPE or HAVE COURAGE TODAY—tosses them into the wind to land somewhere in the street below. Or the man who drops dollar bills into the bushes on his daily walks. The people who receive them may never know where these little gifts have come from, but most likely they will never forget the moment they received it, and chances are they will be moved to do something nice for somebody else.

I give myself the gift of time every month or so—just two or three days—to go to a simple retreat house in the forest about an hour's drive from home. There I rest and meditate and walk silently in the woods, having no contact with the outside world. The Retreat is run by a spiritual order that welcomes anyone who sincerely desires to be in meditative silence for awhile—*for free.* An initial visit to the head teacher to assure him that you are sincere in your desire to rest and be contemplative is the only passport you need for this generous gift of time and space.

Retreatants may not bring work with them, nor electronic devices, and are asked not to leave the property once they arrive; otherwise, we are on our own. The idea is to settle deeply into the silence. After one retreat, I was so grateful for this beautiful place that I broke down as I was leaving and wept in the caretaker's arms. After awhile she said,

"Oh, but you *are* paying for it. Didn't you know? Every hour you sit in contemplation, you are helping to raise the vibrations of the world, and that is what our work is all about."

I think about that everyday. We receive the gifts of the world in order to raise the vibrations of the world. Of course. Treated with generosity, we find it natural and easy to be our finest selves, and we return the favor with our best graciousness and power. At Lynne Twist puns, "What you appreciate, appreciates!"

Right Livelihood

In Buddhist teachings, the Eightfold Path includes the precept of Right Livelihood, which means that the work we do to make a living in the world must be ethical, legal, and create peace among all beings. In today's job market, this is not always easy to come by, especially since so much of what needs doing in the world is the "invisible" work. As a result, having a job to make a living often has little to do with working at what you love to do.

Artists often speak of their "day jobs" to support themselves while staying up all night to write or compose. If they are lucky, these jobs are not soul numbing, but often they are. Some live from hand to mouth—or use food stamps, or the local dumpster—in order to practice their real work without constraints, but this is hard to do when you have responsibilities to others, such as children to support.

Shanti Devi was one woman I knew who took matters into her own hands when the world gave her nothing. She wandered into Kalianpur village in Northern India one day during the year I lived there with my family, begging for food. I was assisting my good friend Dr. Sharan Borwanker, who ran a successful clinic in town but who gave one day per week to work in the surrounding villages to help the women and children of the Ganges plains. Neither of us, of course, was paid by anybody for our work in the villages.

The girl looked to be about 16 years old, pregnant, hungry, and lost. We took her in hand, found her a place to stay and decided that by caring for her we could demonstrate healthy modes of maternity and childcare to the rest of the lower-caste women in the village. Best of all we found her a husband, a young fellow who had recently lost his wife and who worked as a day laborer on a nearby construction project. She would be fed, cared for, and the baby would have a father.

After the baby was born we fitted Shanti Devi with a uterine loop, explaining that it would protect her from another pregnancy until she was ready for a new baby. We hired her to do little jobs for us while her husband was at work, paid her modestly, and taught her about saving money. Each week she would bring us, as her "bank," the few rupees she had saved, and we lavished her with praise, congratulating ourselves as well for our ingenious social experiment.

Then she began appearing more frequently, and with larger sums of money. Soon she was making considerably more than we were! What was going on here? Well, she was smart. Taking our teachings seriously she had put two and two together: a place to stay, contraceptives, and two doctor ladies who made a big fuss every time she brought them her savings. So she set herself up in business, servicing the men working on the construction gang during lunch hour in her empty hut. Oops. ("Business is providing goods and services that people and the earth need ... ")

Not exactly right livelihood, but certainly ingenious. Sharan was appalled, but I laughed (and cried) over it for days. So what is right livelihood, especially in this day and age when an estimated 80 percent of the new generation is educated to do rote jobs that provide little choice about the quality of their lives?

forward." For example, you are waiting to pay your toll on the bridge, when the toll-taker tells you that the car ahead of you has already paid for you, so of course you do the same for the car behind you. Who knows where that chain of forward-payers ends? For the rest of the day, you grin for no reason. Most likely the other drivers do, too.

A local café serves a free Sunday brunch to everyone willing to pay for the people at the next table, and in Philadelphia, one restaurant makes Sunday brunch literally free for any young person who brings in an elder for a meal.

One fellow has taken the idea of Slow Money literally—has stopped it, in fact—by making origami sculptures out of dollar bills to festoon the renovated garbage truck in which he lives.

I have learned about the experiment of equal-value time-sharing from my young friends. One young woman pays for doctor visits by babysitting his child—straight across, hour for hour. They both consider their time equally valuable. In fact, Kait Singley organized that gathering of her peers for me to interview, in exchange for a dance session in my studio. We were both completely satisfied. Computer help may be exchanged for darning socks; garden advice for supper one night. I recently exchanged an herbal tea mixture I had made for colds and flu for all the prunings from a neighbor's lemon verbena plant. We both felt that we'd made a good deal.

Local Economies

In her student days in Berkeley, Gailmarie Kimmel did a weekly Daily Bread run on her bicycle, moving bagels around town, which is how we first met. Her commitment to community activism has followed her to Fort Collins, Colorado, where she has founded the nonprofit organization Buy Local.[14] Its purpose is to reimagine the local economy by fostering independent businesses close to home, keeping hometowns—in this case, Fort Collins—unique. She wants to encourage an economy that is unique to each bioregion and community, expressing its particular flavor and taking advantage of who and what is already there. She starts with the model of a natural ecosystem in which relationship between organisms is taken for granted and every plant and animal contributes to the whole, each species living a healthy life in the context of each other. In her model of community, nothing and nobody is left out, because then everybody and everything would be the poorer for it. And, as she says with a grin, daily life would not be nearly as interesting.

As I write, in early 2010, local currencies are springing up everywhere that complement, not replace, the national economy. One such currency is BerkShares,[15] in the Berkshire Mountains of Massachusetts, which starts with the premise that if there is work that needs doing, and people who are skilled and willing to do that work, skills and goods can be traded directly without the exchange of money. It assumes that the most sustainable economy is one in which the goods and services consumed in a region are produced in the region.

Berkshares also prints up its own currency and collaborates with local banks, businesses, and nonprofits in an alternative economy. Right now, five banks and more than 360 businesses in the area accept their currency, and they are working on expanding their operation to local manufacturers, and to include checking accounts and loans, as well.

In Madison, Wisconsin, the Dane Buy Local[16] organization, whose motto is "Friendly Faces, Neighborhood Places," is also a coalition of one-of-a-kind businesses, local organizations, and individuals who are committed to keeping their economy as close to home as possible. They claim that by supporting local independent business, they are keeping tax dollars in town, providing jobs. Like traditional marketplaces, they are unique and friendly places where shopkeepers and customers get to know each other over time. My friend Rick Brooks, who is on their board, claims that there are more than 400 members now, and the number is growing!

Paring Down

Recently, following my sister's death and the necessity of finding my mother full-time care, I found myself dismantling two households. It was an exhausting, emotional experience, to be sure, but also eye-opening. To begin with, I was finding things I am sure neither my mother nor my sister would have wished me to find, and secondly, I was wading through an unbelievable accumulation of stuff. Every closet and drawer and shelf was packed with clothes and shoes and the litter of decades of enthusiasms, none of which had probably been used in years.

Needless to say, when I had completed both heart-wrenching tasks, I went back home and took stock of my own accumulations and secret embarrassments. And there were plenty of both. I started with our bookshelves, sending several hundred books back into circulation. The local library was delighted to get them for fund-raising book sales, and at home the bookshelves began to breathe. Next, I started on closets, then dresser drawers, then papers. I must have recycled a hundred pounds of manuscript drafts alone, not to mention piles of clothes and everything else that came to light in my search.

I was so exhilarated tossing things into huge bags that my husband demanded he look over the piles to make sure I wasn't getting rid of his favorite sweater. I suggested he go through his closets, too. Pants that had not fit in years, old ties from the days he wore ties, and the contents of file drawers and desk drawers got taken away. It was demented fun, and all the while I was thanking the gods that our children would not have to do this for us.

In fact, I found the process so liberating, I used my next birthday as an excuse for a personal potlatch, telling friends not to bring presents, but to do me the favor of receiving them. For a week, I had a great time deciding which of my no-longer-used treasures would be perfect for which person, then I wrapped them up. It was my favorite birthday in years.

Swaps

All our possessions, all our talents are potentially items for exchange. What is finished for me may well be a new enthusiasm for you, as Wendy Oser proposes twice a year in her Wild Women's Schmata Exchange, where women clean out their closets and swap clothes. Thinking in terms of value rather than market cost, and uninhibited by the need for money, we can all end up rich.

A few years ago, I noticed an ad on a bulletin board suggesting a house swap. The reason given was that the wife was pregnant with their fourth child, and the family lived in a two-bedroom house on a lovely street, with wonderful neighbors, and they could use more space. Was there anyone out there, they wanted to know, who lived in a house too large for them? For example, your own children were grown and gone and you might be interested in moving to their smaller, less expensive house in exchange for your larger, more expensive house. The cost difference, they said, would be negotiated and paid for, and it would all be legally signed and sealed.

That certainly described Herb and me, rattling around in the ramshackle house in which we had raised our three children, and I was intrigued. My mother and my sister were both ill at the time, however, and I already had too much on my plate to consider a complicated move. But it was such an original idea. I wonder if they ever found their match?

I read about another family who sold their home, bought another half the size, and gave the difference to a hunger project in Ghana. Their lives changed radically after that. As the teenage daughter put it: "We set out to make a small difference in the world, but we were the ones transformed in the process."

As wonderful as big swaps are, they do not have to be so momentous; they can be as simple as neighbors taking turns cooking extra servings of a meal and bringing over supper. Childcare exchanges are commonplace in our town, and on our street we water each others' plants and feed each others' cats when someone goes on vacation.

We swap garden tools and ladders, lend each other books and movies, bring over soup when someone gets sick, and know each others' health problems. In our neighborhood, kids' birthday parties take place at the local park, and everyone is welcome. We know the personalities of each others' pets, and most of the children feel comfortable knocking on our doors. It seems so obvious, to live like this. It is called "community," but it might also be called "a cost-effective lifestyle."

Worth and Wealth

While I was carrying out the painful jobs of cleaning out my sister's household, then my mother's, I learned two important things: first, you cannot take anything with you when you die—*not one thing*; and second, your personal treasures are probably not worth all that much to most other people. It was agony for me to watch the way my mother and sister's stuff was pawed over during the estate sales, and I was glad neither of them were there to witness it.

I recently read a study carried out by Derek Bok,[17] former president of Harvard University, on the relationship between income level and happiness. Bok draws attention to the fact that, although the consumption rate has climbed in the United States during the past half-century, people have not become happier as a result: someone called us a nation of "joyless lottery winners." He also wondered why it is that since rising incomes seem not to have made people happier in the past 50 years, we keep working long hours and risking the destruction of our environment just so that we can keep doubling and redoubling our GDP?

In the foreword to Ervin Laszlo's new book, *WorldShift 2012*, well-known spiritual thinker and medical doctor Deepak Chopra[18] addresses this question head on.

He writes:

> *Without a doubt the outmoded world of materialism is leading to greater unhappiness, through pollution, overpopulation, lack of nourishing food and water and the loss of natural habitats; a sizeable percentage of the world's population already experience these deficits. Timely change through a shift in consciousness can bring about a new model of happiness based on the principles of higher consciousness... To the extent that we look outward for happiness, the final result will be boredom, stagnation and bitter disappointment.*

So what is happiness, and what is real wealth, and what has real worth? Clearly, it is not having a big pot of money in the bank. President Theodore Roosevelt once said that real wealth was that which benefited the whole community. This description makes sense to me. It is children cherished and fed; it is old people warm in the winter, as Brendan Behan used to say. It is a healthy natural world around us, and enough to eat and the pleasures of eating it together. It is water we can drink and swim in, and work that is meaningful, and love, and getting along with each other even when we don't love each other so much. It is dreaming up new things and creating beauty and having bright ideas and laughing a lot.

Among hunter-gatherers like the Penan people in Borneo, wealth is explicitly understood as consisting of the relative strength of relations among people because everyone in the tribe is dependent upon everyone else for survival. If the group splits because people are not getting along, then everyone starves, so solidarity is the priority in their culture.

Wealth and worth and value is, more than anything, this precious opportunity we have each been given to be alive in the world right this minute. We're here NOW. Our life won't last forever. There's not a moment to waste.

The insurance industry makes a profound mistake when, in its own terminology, it refers to our miraculous, unpredictable, beautiful, and terrible world as an "attractive nuisance." We know better. We understand that this is our chance to be in human bodies and to experience "the whole enchilada" of the world in all its vagaries and wonders. We live off the land, and we must recognize that fact, even if we live in a concrete high-rise in a great city. Being alive is our chance to learn and explore, make mistakes and rejoice, be surprised and be grateful. Value comes from living well; wealth derives from the opportunity to do so, from spending the treasure of time with generosity and deep joy.

Money? What's that?

La luna es moneda lustrosa
en el alcancía de la noche,
ahorro del dormir
para gastar prodigiosamente
en sueños.

The moon is a lustrous coin in the bank of the night,
Savings of sleep to spend prodigiously
On dreams.
—*RAFAEL JESUS GONZALEZ, POET*

ADDITIONAL INSPIRATIONS

The Money Fix is a documentary available on DVD that examines economic patterning in both the human and the natural worlds. Through this lens, we learn how we can empower ourselves by reorganizing the lifeblood of the economy at the community level. The film documents three types of alternative money systems, all of which help solve economic problems for the communities in which they operate. For more information, visit *www.themoneyfix.org*

Katherine Neville has written a wonderful page-turner of a novel, *A Calculated Risk* (Ballantine Books 1992) about corruption in the banking system.

Positive News from Around the World is a good-news newspaper now appearing in the UK and the US, that is dedicated to printing news that creates a positive future. Its articles are stories of the environment, sustainable energy, education, what our youth are doing, etc. For more information, visit *www.positivenews.com* or *www.positivenews.org.uk*

Organizations in which some of the young people I interviewed are involved:
Zelig Golden and **Julie Wolk**: *www.WildernessTorah.org*
Caitlin Sislin: *www.womensearthalliance.org*
Abram Katz and **Sarah Minarik**: *www.indigitalkids.org*
K. Ruby Blume *www.iuoakland.com*

The Kogi, **Wiwa**, and **Arhuaco** peoples of the Colombian highlands made the following joint declaration in January 2004:

> *Who will pay the universal mother for the air we breathe, the water that flows, the light of the sun? Everything that exists has a spirit that is sacred and must be respected. Our law is the law of origins, the law of life. We invite all the Younger Brothers to be guardians of life. We affirm our promise to the Mother, and issue a call for solidarity and unity for all peoples and all nations.*

ENDNOTES

1. **Ervin László** was born 1932 in Budapest, Hungary and currently lives in Tuscany, Italy. A philosopher of science, a systems theorist, and a classical pianist, the focus of his work is on the Worldshift we are now globally experiencing. For more information, visit *http://en.wikipedia.org/wiki/Ervin_László*

2. **Braden R. Allenby** is currently professor of Civil and Environmental Engineering, and of Law, at Arizona State University. For more information, visit *http://webapp4.asu.edu/directory/person/744560*

3. **The Daily Bread Project** is an urban gleaning project in Berkeley, California, that picks up surplus food from food businesses and brings the food to free feeding sites around the Bay Area. It was founded in 1983 and is still run entirely by volunteers. To find out more about Daily Bread and how to start your own, visit *www.healingimprovisations.net/social/dailybread.htm*

4. **Martín Prechtel** has been a Mayan shaman, a scholar, teacher, author, painter, and musician. He gives workshops in many parts of the world and teaches a course called "Bolad's Kitchen" at his home in New Mexico. For more information, visit *www.floweringmountain.com*

5. **The Soul of Money Institute** was founded in 2003 by Lynne Twist. It is a center for exploring and sharing the best practices, theories, and attitudes that enable people to relate to money and the money culture with greater freedom and effectiveness. For more information, visit *www.soulofmoney.org*

6. **Wade Davis** is an ethnographer, writer, photographer, filmmaker, and ethnobotanist, He spent more than three years in the Amazon and Andes as a plant explorer, living among 15 indigenous groups in eight Latin American nations while making some 6,000 botanical collections. His work later took him to Haiti to investigate folk preparations implicated in the creation of zombies, For more information, visit *http://www.nationalgeographic.com/field/explorers/wade-davis.html*

7. **Inverness Valley Inn** on the Point Reyes Peninsula in Northern California honors the earth by using green practices, including solar electricity generation, a saline pool, earth-friendly amenities and cleaning products, green laundry operations, organic coffees and teas, and more. The owners are Alden and Leslie Adkins. For more information, visit *www.invernessvalleyinn.com*

8.   **Craigslist** is an online listing of local classified ads in the United States, providing forums for jobs, housing, personal services, and events. For more information visit *www.craigslist.org*

9.   **Joanna Macy** is an eco-philosopher and scholar of Buddhism, general systems theory, and deep ecology. She interweaves Buddhism with social activism and teaches around the world. For more information, visit *www.joannamacy.net*

10. **The Center for Safe Energy (CSE)** has been fostering citizen exchanges between the former Soviet Union and the United States, especially of environmental activists, since 1989. For more information, visit *http://eii.org/eiproject/index.php/cse/*

11. **Slow Money** was founded by Woody Tasch to build local and national networks dedicated to investing in small food enterprises and local food systems, connecting investors to their local economies and building the nurture capital industry. For more information visit *www.slowmoneyalliance.org*

12. **Jane Jacobs** (May 4, 1916 – April 25, 2006) was an American-born Canadian writer and activist whose primary interest was in communities and urban planning and decay. For more information, visit *http://en.wikipedia.org/wiki/Jane_Jacobs*

13. **Catherine Austin Fitts** is the president of Solari, Inc. and managing member of Solari Investment Advisory Services, LLC. For more information, visit *http://solari.com/*

14. **Gailmarie Kimmel** is an environmental educator in Fort Collins, Colorado, who enjoys reimagining the economy. She is the founder of BUY LOCAL. For more information, visit *www.belocalnc.org/gailmarie-kimmel*

15. **BerkShares** is a local currency for the Berkshire region of Massachusetts. Dubbed a "great economic experiment" by the *New York Times*, BerkShares is a tool for community empowerment, enabling merchants and consumers to plant the seeds for an alternative economic future for their communities. For more information, visit *www.berkshares.org*.

16. **Dane Buy Local** is a coalition of local independent businesses, organizations, and citizens in and around Dane County, Wisconsin, that is acting in alliance to keep their communities prosperous and sustainable. For more information, visit *www.danebuylocal.com*

17. **Derek Bok** is the 300th anniversary university research professor and university president emeritus of Harvard University in Cambridge, Massachsetts. To learn more about his views on happiness and the economy, please visit *www.charlierose.com/view/content/10988*

18. **Deepak Chopra, M.D.**, is a world-renowned authority in the field of mind-body healing, a best-selling author, and co-founder of the Chopra Center for Wellbeing. A global force in the field of human empowerment, Dr. Chopra is the prolific author of more than 55 books, including 14 bestsellers on mind-body health, quantum mechanics, spirituality, and peace. For more information, visit *www.chopra.com*

CHAPTER TWO

FOOD

THE ALLIGATORS' SONG

We're the top of the food chain,
Ain't Nature grand.
We're makin' a menu –
Cookin' a band.
Bite-sized pieces, juicy chunks,
Crispy niblets, tender hunks.
Plucking, skinning, poaching, frying,
Roasting, basting – and Oh yes, dying…
But never mind, don't yield to fright,
It's all over in one bite –
At the top of the food chain,
Ain't Nature grand,
Ain't Nature grand!

—FROM MAMA DON'T ALLOW

MUSIC AND LYRICS BY JULIE SHEARER

In 1983, my husband was invited to Fudan University in Shanghai to give lectures on chemistry and physics to help Chinese scientists catch up after the Cultural Revolution. I went along to teach English conversation in the Modern Language Department, and we lived across from the campus in faculty housing. Our meals were prepared for us at a guesthouse a short walk from our place; they were simple and delicious. The cook and I became friends, and I often joined her in the kitchen to watch her cook.

On the morning of an official banquet held in our honor, we sent a note to the kitchen saying we would forego breakfast that day, after being warned that a Chinese banquet can often run to 15 courses. That morning we lounged around the apartment, took a rare bath, and planned to go on a long walk before the mixed pleasures of all that food. I had been told to expect shark's fin soup, whole ducks, fish, and many varieties of pork with vegetables. We wanted to be *very* hungry by the time we got there.

There was a tapping at our door—quite unexpected, as it was still a time in China when foreigners were out of bounds for the Chinese—and there stood the cook from the guesthouse, beaming and bearing a tray loaded with various breakfast foods in duplicate. With gestures and the few words we had learned to exchange, she explained that since we had not come down for breakfast, she was bringing it to us instead!

Dumplings and fried bread, rice gruel with bits of smoked meat, even pork chops! "Eat!" she commanded with a broad smile. "You like?" We had little choice but to eat. Our Mandarin was almost nonexistent, and our reasons for not wanting breakfast, complex. After her kindly ongoing efforts for us, we could hardly turn her down. In agony, we ate everything.

My memory of the banquet later in the day was that it continued well into the evening, the food was fabulous even beyond our expectations, and by the third course I wanted to die.

Food Properties

It is a human instinct to be generous with guests even when you have little to eat yourself. In many places, families will share with the newcomer even when they have almost no food themselves. For our banquet in China, the table groaned beneath an abundance of food that was designed to compliment and impress us, as well as feed us. I recall being surrounded by waiters ready to respond to our every request, which meant they had to witness our every mouthful.

In the Sahara, I have heard, if a guest shows up hungry at their tent, people expect to slaughter their last goat—even if the milk of that very goat is what they feed to their children. Knowing this made it hard for me to swallow down the delicacies I was being served, and I wondered if, at the very least, the people waiting on us got to go home with our leftovers.

Probably not, as I had painfully learned when we lived in India. Our bungalow in the Ganges Plain came with servants: a cook, a sweeper, and an *ayah*, or nanny, for the children. Our cook, Chottey Lal, was a proud man who refused to believe that I did my own cooking when I was at home in America. "My own cleaning and gardening and childcare, too," I would tell him. "Oh no, *memsahib*," he would declare, certain I was joking with him.

I had asked him to cook us an ordinary North Indian diet, leaving out only the hottest spices. Each morning, I would request about twice the amount I expected our family to eat, assuming that the rest would return to the kitchen and be taken out the back door to his quarters, a single concrete room where he lived with his two grown children.

One evening after dinner I happened to go into the kitchen, where I saw him tossing the leftovers into the trash. I must have shrieked because I remember the scene that followed being painful for both of us.

"Chottey Lal," I gasped, "that food is for you!"

"No *memsahib*," he announced, rising to his full height and standing before me, proud, "that is rich man food. If God wanted me to each rich man food, he would make me a rich man. A poor man eat poor man food."

A few days later I asked him if I could go with him to the market, hoping to talk with him about it. He very reluctantly agreed. Once there in the jostling crowd, I asked questions about different foods I didn't recognize and picked up vegetables that looked good and plopped them into our basket.

He was resigned, but when I picked out one particular bunch of greens, he balked.

"This poor man food," he insisted. Tentatively, I put it into the basket anyway. He shook his head. Then I got obstinate, saying I wanted to taste it, and he sighed with displeasure.

That night I asked him to cook those greens for supper, and his face went stony. I heard a lot of clanging in the kitchen, and when I looked in, a huge cooking pot was bubbling away, water up to the brim, the greens dissolving into green foam. It boiled, I think, for most of an hour, and when he brought it to the table, it was a revolting mess of greenish slime. Haughty and expressionless, he spooned it out.

"Chottey Lal," I said quietly as it sloshed over the rims of our plates, "we cannot eat this."

"That's what I told you, *memsahib*!" he responded with dignity. "It poor man food!"

Chottey Lal lived by the assumptions of his caste society, unacceptable to this 29-year-old American woman, but unlike me at the time, or many of us now, he knew where his food came from. He even grew it in the narrow strip of dirt between our back door and his tiny hovel, and sold his produce to the vegetable *walla* who made the rounds to our front doors with his pushcart. Once, when he discovered that I had bought squash from the *walla* that he, Chottey Lal, had grown, he was so disappointed he sputtered that he would have given it to me, had he known I wanted it.

We may well ask: where does food come from and who gets to eat what? What is healthy to eat, and what is toxic? How do we sustain its production, and how do we make sure there is enough to go around?

Facts And Figures

- In 2006, the population of the United States was 300 million people, too large for our current farmland and food system to keep up with.
- 800 million people in the world are chronically underfed.
- 40,000 children die of starvation in the world everyday.
- Historically, people have eaten 80,000 plant species; currently, three-quarters of all our food in the United States comes from eight plant species.
- All the important crops we now eat were domesticated about 5,000 years ago.
- We are currently using a billion pounds of petro-chemicals each year to control insects and weeds, creating dead zones in and around large agricultural fields.
- More than 500 insect species are now resistant to the insecticides developed to kill them; the same applies to weeds and herbicides.
- In the United States, more than 5,000 people die annually from chemicals put into processed food to make it free from pathogens.
- Organic, unsprayed produce contains considerably higher levels of antioxidants, flavonoids, and vitamins than chemically treated produce.

- Eggs from free-range chickens have more vitamin E, beta-carotene, omega-3 fatty acids, as well as half the cholesterol of factory-farmed eggs.
- Livestock grown for meat accounts for 37 percent of the methane and 65 percent of the nitrous oxide in the atmosphere, (greenhouse gasses more potent than carbon dioxide.)
- 90 percent of federal subsidies go to Big Agriculture crops rather than to small family farms.

The Food Chain

The natural world is a society where nothing is wasted in the food chain. Everything is food for everything else, dead or alive, from microscopic bacteria to omnivores like us at the top of the food chain. This was graphically brought home to me one day on the Galapagos Islands, that world of lava and sand, sea and sky, where each of the rare species, plant and animal, stands out in stark relief against black volcanic rock. A dead sea lion lay on the beach, swarming with frenzied flies feeding and laying their eggs in its rotting flesh. Lava lizards darted after the flies, mockingbirds pecked at the writhing maggots, and hawks swooped to swallow the lava lizards. It was a movable feast, the dead sea lion being quickly resurrected through the bodies of everyone else around.

Just as there are interconnections among the flies, lizards, and birds and their food, in this case a dead sea lion, so too is there an intimate relationship between the eater and the thing that is eaten. We are all part of a living web of life and merge with each other, just as the lava lizards physically merged with the hawks who swallowed them. As Michael Pollan,[1] author of *The Omnivore's Dilemma*, points out: "Eating puts us in touch with all that we share with other animals, and all that sets us apart. It defines us." Therefore, it is a good idea to know what we are eating and where it comes from.

Mark Sommer, host of the radio show interview series *A World of Possibilities*, made a game of this with his daughter Maya every evening at dinner. "Where did this carrot, this fish, this salad come from?" he would ask, and together they would trace its journey from the source to their plates. He said he learned as much as she did.

Wendy Johnson,[2] fabulous gardener and author of *Gardening at the Dragon's Gate*, claims that we ought to even know the faces of the farmers who grow our food. "No anonymous food!" she says vehemently. These days, there are several ways of doing this that are available to most of us, wherever we live.

Farmers Markets and CSAs

Farmers markets,[3] where farmers come into the city with their produce from the country along with breads and honey and olive oil and fish and almost everything else you might hanker for (in season), have been springing up everywhere—even in Alaska! Other stalls sell produce grown locally, in the city, and some sell exotic prepared foods for shoppers to munch as they do their marketing. In our town, I can shop at one farmers market on Tuesday in one location, on Saturday in another, and on Sunday in yet a third, and each is within five minutes of where I live. I know which farmer grows the best purple potatoes and whose eggs have the most orange yolks. I make a point of buying from several farmers, rather than getting everything I need at just one or two stalls, because I enjoy getting to know them all over time. We exchange news about how the cold snap has affected the tomatoes and zucchini, and we talk about ways to sweeten the rhubarb. Once, after I had been traveling, the farmer from whom I always bought my broccoli and cauliflower called out, "Hey, you been away? Haven't seen you for awhile."

The markets are like parties: everyone you know is there, musicians line the paths, every booth offers tastes, and the kids walk around with strawberries and tomatoes smeared all over their faces. It often happens that I meet up with just the people I've been meaning to call, so I always figure in an extra hour in my schedule when I go to the market. It is reassuring to know that whatever I buy there was picked that morning, had not traveled hundreds of miles to reach me, and was grown in healthy soil undepleted by a cocktail of chemicals. Wendy claims that at farmers' markets we exchange more than good food and farming advice; we create fresh culture and community on common ground, meeting face to face over local produce.

If you live in the city, work long hours, and getting to the market is a chore, there might be a metropolitan buyers club near you. Here, you order in advance what you want to buy, it gets delivered to a dropoff point near you, and you pick up a box of produce once a week.

Or there might be a Community-Supported Agriculture (CSA)[4] farm near you that you can join. CSAs were started in Japan in 1965 by mothers concerned about pesticides in their food and the corresponding decrease in farm production. They called their movement *Teikei*, which means "food with a farmer's face on it." At a CSA, everybody pays a set amount at the beginning of the season, thereby providing capital for the farmer to plant his or her fields. As each crop becomes ripe, CSA shareholders reap the harvest with boxes of produce that arrive weekly at a pickup place in each neighborhood. Normally, the boxes arrive with recipes and suggestions of how to prepare the veggies contained within, a newsletter, and invitations to visit the farm. Hoe Downs, the parties held at the Full Belly Farm[5] in October each year, when farm and farmers take a rest after the pumpkin season is over, is one of the best parties I know, especially for the kids. Children who have had so much fun at a farm will never turn down their vegetables! The only problem I have ever had with my CSA experience is overabundance, and trying to figure out what to do with so much cabbage when the cabbages are in!

Putting Food By

My daughter Rebecca, who is a volunteer harvester at a CSA outside Boston, Massachusetts, says, "Put it by! While the cabbages are at their peak, and you cannot eat another bite of cole slaw, make sauerkraut."

She suggests you can it and give it out as holiday gifts. If it's apples, make applesauce; when it's chard, cook it up and freeze it. You can put up peach jam, apricot preserves, plum chutney, tomato sauce, cucumber pickles, the list goes on … My own favorites include lemon sorbet, when lemons are falling off the trees around here, and stewed pears, and every year I put up quantities of tomatoes and freeze mounds of pesto when the basil comes in. A dinner of pasta with pesto and tomato sauce in the middle of winter is a treat and can be whipped up in minutes, and canned fruit always provides a homemade dessert, ready to go. At our house, the jars lining the shelves are our fast-food source. They are so beautiful, gleaming like fruity jewels, and are available all year long.

We share a backyard with our neighbors, as well as a mature Gravenstein apple tree that produces bushels of apples each year. We all start harvesting the windfalls as early as mid-August, and are still picking fruit off the tree at the end of September. Todd, our next-door neighbor, makes terrific apple pies and I, during those apple-filled weeks, am constantly putting up applesauce from the windfalls. Between us we make enough apple-related goodies to last well into the winter. And when the wild plum starts to drop its fruit, Todd and nine-year-old Tristan make the sweetest jam together!

I put up cucumber pickles one year with another neighbor, Meg, who is a perfectionist. My own style is rather slapdash, and she is often exasperated by my casual approach. However, we thought we could do this task together, and indeed, we could. But when the long slices were tucked into their tall jars and the brine poured and the lids sealed, we stood back to admire our handiwork and then had hysterics. In her jars, each spear was parallel to the next, little green soldiers neatly standing side by side. My jars were recognizable by their helter-skelter mayhem, seeds floating and tips smashed flat. Once pickled, however, we did a taste test, and she had to admit that mine tasted just as good as hers, even though hers were definitely classier.

Mostly, I like to do our canning and freezing with family, friends, and neighbors and make a party of it. But it's just as easy to do on your own, a little bit at a time. When you are shopping, you pick up an extra few pounds of tomatoes or peaches, or whatever is at its peak at the time, and plop them into a pot while you are preparing dinner that night. It cooks up while you are eating, and afterward may take another 20 minutes or so to spoon it into containers—recycled yogurt containers work fine. Then you tuck them into the freezer, "putting up the harvest like it's going out of season," which it is.

Make a load of pesto in the summer, when basil is abundant, or salsa, when tomatoes and spices are abundant, and —you can spoon it into ice-cube trays for individual servings during the winter. Same with fruit juice, for the children—with toothpicks they make terrific popsicles.

Cheese, of course, is a way of putting milk by; wine is one way to put the grape harvest by. Apples go into cider, and oranges go into marmalade. There is virtually no end to the possibilities.

Gleaning and Gathering

There are farms and orchards surrounding many suburbs where people are welcome to come pick their own produce, and it makes for a wonderful Sunday outing. When our children were growing up, we had our favorite country lanes and orchards where we went, in season, for blackberries and whatever other fruit was in season. We'd set out with a big picnic and many buckets and baskets, returning home at night itching and smeared purple, with untold pounds of blackberries for jams and pies.

Bulk buying among neighbors is another inexpensive way of stocking up on staples: flours, grains, nuts, and beans. One person orders from the warehouse, everybody pays a share, and you get together to redistribute it, sometimes having a potluck dinner together as well.

For years, our local volunteer food-running organization, Daily Bread,[6] has done this directly with one farmer who periodically delivers a truckload of rice and beans to our "depot," a church basement in the middle of town. Every few months we throw a bagging party open to parishioners, our own volunteers, and anybody else willing to spend a few hours filling paper bags with one-pound portions of rice and beans. These bags are later distributed to folks who need it. The parties always remind me of quilting bees, where we gossip and tell stories while we fill bag after bag, and the kids run around and eat cookies the church women have put out, and someone sits on the sidelines strumming a guitar.

Meal sharing is an obvious antidote to the daily meal-preparation crunch, which few of us take advantage of. It is simple to make a bigger pot of soup, or two casseroles instead of one when you are cooking up dinner on, say, Tuesdays, and bring your surplus to a nearby friend or neighbor for their dinner. Then they do the same for you on, say, Fridays. Or maybe your neighbors are up to their necks in full-time jobs, two kids, and illness in the family; maybe another is elderly and living alone. In either case, the gift of food is welcome and always heartwarming. Maybe they cannot reciprocate directly but then, one Sunday, you may find an apple pie at your doorstep, or a pot of soup. Nothing bonds people like sharing food, and if you are cooking anyway, it is the easiest thing in the world to do.

Where my brother lives in Vermont, friends of his have been holding a monthly potluck supper for the last 30 years. I have been to many of these, as I visit there as often as I can. The most memorable potluck I've been to—and one that still makes me chuckle—was held in late August at the height of zucchini season, when dinner consisted of zucchini casserole, zucchini ratatouille, stuffed zucchini, grated zucchini fritters, and zucchini slices fried in batter. As they warned me, "You'd better lock your car or somebody will dump their zucchini in the back seat!"

Big Ag

We've come a long way since the 1950s, when my parents felt sorry for the Woizniches up the street, an elderly Polish couple who "couldn't afford canned peas and carrots and had to grow their own in their backyard, instead." For us first-generation Americans, anything that smacked of Old Country poverty, what my parents called "just off the boat," was to be avoided at all costs, and packaged food was a sign of prosperity. I wonder if Industrial Agriculture got its boost from those families who, just one generation away from Old Country *peasants*, wanted so badly to be modern Americans?

Industrial Agriculture, also called Agribusiness or Big Ag, refers to corporate ownership of huge tracts of land on which a single crop is grown. Monoculture is notoriously prone to attracting pests. This means huge amounts of pesticides must be used, which of course depletes the soil, which then requires industrial fertilizer for the next year's crop. As herbicides have gotten rid of all the weeds, beneficial and otherwise, the fields are laid bare after each harvest; this is no doubt the major cause of the 24 billion tons of topsoil that are lost worldwide every year.

I remember when my husband and I first drove crosscountry from east to west in the early 1960s, driving through mile after mile of cornfields in the Midwest. There were rustling green rows, at every stage of growth, as far as the eye could see in every direction. We stopped at a diner in one farming town, looking forward to some of the freshest corn we had ever tasted, and we were served canned niblets! I was shocked and asked if we could have some of the corn growing right outside the back of the diner instead. The waitress laughed and said, "We don't eat that stuff; that's for hogs!" In that moment, I came of age.

Small Family Farms

Industrial farms are the antithesis of the small family farm model, in which a family lives on the land it tills. It produces a variety of crops and food animals that do well in that particular bioregion, and the farm family is an integral part of the surrounding community.

One of the advantages of producing huge volumes of a crop may be that the price you pay at the supermarket is relatively low, but the *cost* we all pay—the erosion of soil, the polluted air and water, the loss of natural fertility and biodiversity, the disruption of community—is incalculable. We may finally be recognizing this fact. (The main advantage of this kind of agriculture probably has to do with CEO's salaries anyway, and little to do with the rest of us.) Michael Pollan, author of *The Botany of Desire*, tells us that our food system depends on consumers being ignorant of all the embodied costs that go into the food they pay for. "Cheapness and ignorance are mutually reinforcing," he says.

In Ireland, the monoculture of a single variety of potato eventually resulted in a massive famine; in India, the promises of the Green Revolution are rapidly coming apart as the land withers under all those chemicals. For awhile, crops grow like gangbusters and feed hordes more people, but in the long haul Nature rebels, and the earth is compromised. Which means that *we all* are compromised—plants, animals, and humans. For we and all living systems are connected to each other and to the earth, whether we know it or not. That's the way Nature works. No miraculous high technology can change that—even genetic engineering. Michael Pollan warns us that at both ends of the food chain is a biological system—a patch of soil, a human body— and the health of one is connected to the health of the other. Period.

The Locavore[7] and Slow Food[8] Movements

Many people recently have been experimenting with purchasing only what is locally produced within a radius of some number of miles from where they live, and limiting their diets to what is locally available. Many are trying it out for a year, say, as writer Barbara Kingsolver describes in her wonderful book *Animal, Vegetable, Miracle*. They call themselves *Locavores* a word that was named, in 2007, the "Word of the Year" by the New Oxford American Dictionary. Locavore is defined as a "collaborative, locally based, self-reliant food economy—sustainable production, processing, distribution and consumption—which enhances the economic, environmental and social health of a community."

As Virginia farmer and activist Joel Salatin, owner of Polyface Farm,[9] says: "The yearning in the human soul to smell a flower, pet a pig and enjoy food with a face has never been stronger." If we can produce our own food very close to home, all the better. And if we consume only what we can grow ourselves—making us what might be called "Yokelvores"—better still.

Eating locally also implies eating seasonally. Since strawberries do not grow in New Hampshire in the middle of the winter, if you want strawberry shortcake to be a traditional part of your New Year's Day brunch, then you have an alternative to buying strawberries shipped halfway around the world to your supermarket in December. Put them by! Get yourself a lug of strawberries in the summer, when they are plentiful and ripe, cook them up (ah, the aroma!), and store them for spectacular winter eating. Or you might freeze them and bag them, for winter cooking. Pleasure in the spring; pleasure in the winter. It will wow your friends!

For most of us, being a locavore means that we learn the practices of the grocery stores we shop in: which ones buy from local farmers; where fish caught locally on handlines is sold; where you can buy locally raised free-range chickens. You'd be surprised, no matter where you live, how many of these enterprises are popping up. Even the White House[10]—thank you, Michelle Obama—now has its own organic garden.

Slow Food, not the same but similar to Locavore in intent, was started in Italy in 1989 when a McDonald's opened in Rome near the Spanish Steps and the local defenders of Italy's traditional food culture raised the roof. No homogenized, bland, boring food for them! The cry has been taken up in local chapters, or conviviums, all over the world in support of local, traditional ways of eating.

It reminds me of a long train ride I took in the late 1950s, when I was a student in France. I was going to spend Christmas with my Italian boyfriend and his family in Ravenna, Italy. I shared a seat with a Frenchman also going home for the holidays, and we struck up a conversation about our lives, as people do on trains. When he got off at his stop in the south of France, he called over his shoulder,

"*Adieu mon amie*! You are on your way to eat spaghetti, *et moi*, I am going home to eat *la bouillabaisse*!"

Slow food, I think, is about the pleasure of growing, preparing, and sharing food. The poet and farmer Wendell Berry[11] says that eating is an agricultural act, and I would add that along with being a biological act, it is also a social act, a cultural act, and an emotional act.

Home Foods

I will never forget that Christmas in Ravenna. Madly in love with the son of the family, Franco, I helped make the traditional *capelletti*, the stuffed pasta made once a year for Christmas in the Emilia region of Italy. Along with Mamma and Franco's two sisters, I wore a kerchief knotted around my hair and we all had on tomato-smeared aprons as we rolled out the dough. We cut it into little squares, scooped a dab of meat filling into each square and then, with a deft twist of the wrist—one I never quite managed to achieve—rolled and twisted each bundle into a tiny "hat." Meanwhile, *mio* Franco, whose cello music made me weak in the knees, played for us in the next room. His Pappa, Babbo, I recall, stood in the hallway between the kitchen and bedroom, beaming at the *delicioso* scene in his home. Aromas of cooking food, four of his favorite women working together, the sounds of Boccherini coming from his gifted son, and the anticipation of the Christmas meal to come. Ahh.

Home Grown

My brother and his family have a small farm in Vermont, where the growing season is measured in weeks. They manage to produce much of their own food by extending the season with greenhouses, canning much of what they grow, and piling winter vegetables in bins all over the place. Carrots, onions, parsnips, and potatoes line the mudroom of their old farmhouse, and under the beds can be found bushels of winter squash, seeds, more onions and garlic, and jars of maple syrup. I love going there.

During one visit, everyone was down with a winter cold, so I offered to make a chicken soup for the family. At the Putney Co-Op, I bought a locally raised chicken (I even happened to know the farmer) and, without thinking, purchased all the other ingredients from the produce section, not noticing that much of it came from California. Back at the farm when I unpacked the chicken, carrots, onions, and parsnips, my sister-in-law had a fit of laughing and coughing, pointing out to me the bushels of carrots, parsnips, and onions sitting in the mud-room just outside the kitchen door. From their own soil, their own hands, and I had missed it!

Ultimately, growing food in good soil is about our health, the plants' health, and the soil's health. When crops come from toxic, depleted soil that requires chemicals and genetically modified seeds to grow, and animals are packed into cages and feedlots only for the purpose of providing food for our species, then something is inherently out of whack with the system. We buy vitamins as if our lives depended on them and teach our children about food groups, but rather than making us healthy, many of us are overfed and undernourished. As Pollan reminds us, "We are a notably unhealthy people obsessed by the idea of eating healthily."

It is changing now. Community gardens are happening in cities everywhere, and urban gardens—even "farms" with poultry—are being dug, like the old victory gardens during World War Two—only now the "victory" is in health and beauty and the great pleasure of working the earth and eating the bounty.

Backyard lawns are being taken out and converted to beds we plant with food crops and perennial flowers; window-boxes are showing up on porches and fire escapes; sidewalk strips outside people's houses are being planted with greens and potatoes. People are even planting miniature indoor gardens,[12] growing what one gardener calls microgreen blends for quick harvest. These kitchen-window planters grow mesclun, or an assortment of greens meant to be picked young for salads.

We are falling in love with our little gardens. As master gardener Wendy Johnson says, "I have a garden, and the garden has me!"

My friend Enrique Sanchez tells me about the opuntia cactus growing in his front yard. "Opuntia is a staple food in Mexico," he writes, "and is known as *nopales*. Mexico exports tons of it from a place not far from where I was born, and the fruit, known as cactus pears, or *punas,* are tasty. My parents love them, and I always bring some over." He says that neighbors often knock on his door, and he is glad to share his harvest with whoever comes a'knocking. When the harvest is big, he fills bags of nopales and drops them off in places where he knows they will be appreciated. Just last night he brought over a homemade pizza of nopales and cheese. Delicious! I love drive-bys …

For years, until the city authorities finally carted it away, the Ecocity founder Richard Register[13] had an ancient convertible filled with soil and brimming with vegetables and flowers parked in front of his house. He called it "The Vegetable Car." Planters are being made from toilet bowls and old sinks, hubcaps and wine barrels—anything that will hold some soil and support a plant. We are starting to hoe down everywhere, in the city as well as in the country, and we are loving it!

Permaculture Design

The word "permaculture"[14] didn't exist before 1959, when Bill Mollison of Australia coined it to refer to a way of restoring damaged land ecologically, the way Nature does it. His premise was that monoculture, row crops, the clearing of forests, the diverting of streams, and paving over of the land misunderstood the interconnections in a healthy ecosystem, leading to a degradation of all life, including ours.

The American permaculturalist Toby Hemenway,[15] author of my favorite book on permaculture, *Gaia's Garden*, claims that restoring the earth begins in our own gardens, however large or small and wherever we live. Everything works together from the ground up to yield food, flowers, and herbs for people while providing habitat for insects, birds, and wildlife.

Mother Earth is a *both/and* enterprise not an *either/or* battle. As gardeners, we can take care of our small plots of Earth as part of a whole ecology, related to the air and water that we all share, and the well-being of the flying creatures and the crawling ones who pay no attention to our property lines. By doing so, we can help to restore the Eden that our world, in fact, is.

The ecological designer John Todd[16] suggests that we create our gardens in the image of a meadow: we initiate the process and then let it evolve as it will. Nature knows what to do, once we help create the conditions. "Let Nature do it!" is the hue and cry of the permaculture movement, an idea that requires a lot less backbreaking and complicated work from the gardener. The mantra goes like this:

"Use what is there. Don't do so much backbreaking work. Don't be so neat."
It's all about the soil, we are told, and most of the work is about restoring the soil.

The Home Soil

I'm one of those people who loves dirt. It is, after all, literally the ground of our being. There's something about the smell of wet soil in the spring that makes me glad to be alive. Soil has been called the "ecstatic skin of the earth." That speaks to me, so every spring I go out to the local horse stables with buckets and bags and tarps to collect mulch from their rich piles of manure and straw, which are free for the taking. I come home elated and filthy, smelling of good, aged horseshit, then I spread it on the garden, happy as a clam. Dark gold.

Grass clippings, composted leaves, bales of straw, coffee grounds, and compost from the worm bin all find their mulchy way into the garden, which, over the years, has turned our clay soil from hardpan into rich, friable loam teeming with earthworms. The biologist E. O. Wilson[17] has said that there are more microorganisms in a cup of healthy soil than there are human beings on Earth. Something in me knows that, and there have been times when, checking first to make sure nobody is watching, I'll scoop up a handful and bury my nose in it and even take a taste.

Can you imagine making a garden without hours of backbreaking digging? With mega-mulch, you can. Permaculture gardens are not dug *into* the ground but built *on top of* the ground, with layer after layer of mulch. Like making a giant lasagna, you lay down biodegradable cardboard first—to discourage the lawn or weedlot from further growth—and on top of that you place layer after layer of leaves and manure, straw and compost, wood chips, and worm casings. Then you sprinkle your lasagna with cover crop seeds (instead of cheese) and the seeds of whatever other plants you like to eat, using open-pollinated seeds as much as possible so that the plants can reseed themselves. Then you let it "cook." Some food plants—peas, for example, and tomatoes—do best if you start them from nursery seedlings tucked into a hole in the mulch. (Make sure the hole goes all the way through the cardboard to the earth layer.) It gives them a bit of a head start. If you think that sounds too easy, just try it.

Plant roots know what to do: they thread their way down into the undisturbed topsoil beneath your mulch layers and find their way to water. You've created a self-organizing ecology that is self-fertilizing and has internal weed suppression and moisture control. And as the seasons change, the potatoes and radishes, collards and fava beans, peas and tomatoes, cucumbers and onions and garlic you plant will make their appearance. So will squash and pumpkins, as well as unexpected volunteers from your compost pile, and wind-borne seeds. Get ready with stakes and trellises for the vines!

When volunteer plants take root, watch out for the errant avocado or plum tree seedling and snip it at its base leaving the roots to mulch in the ground. Or dig it out, roots and all, and make little gifts to your friends for their gardens. Make sure, though, that you have not inadvertently left a tree to grow where you only have a small planting space. Like weeds, some volunteers can be the most tenacious plants in the garden, so if they are not what you want there, learn what they look like and deal with them before their root systems become too established. I'll never forget how hard we worked on the elderberry tree that had put down two deep taproots while I'd been assuming it was just a very healthy chard.

Weeds

As an Eastern European Jew whose forebears have been systematically weeded out of societies all over the world for as long as there is written history, I am protective toward weeds. They inevitably are the plants that want to grow where they are, and they do it much more hardily than the exotics I might have chosen for that place. Permaculturalists are wont to say they cannot understand why folks spend so much time killing plants that want to grow, and growing plants that want to die!

Weeds are seasonal, local, and free. Many are edible, herbal, or medicinal and, often show up exactly where that particular species is needed by the inhabitants nearby. It's not a bad idea to note what pesky weed keeps popping up in your garden and then check out its medicinal properties. It might be just what you need.

A few years ago, I decided to turn our small backyard into a weed garden. The front yard is where we grow our food, but I refer to the backyard as our Medicinal Herb Garden, to give it a touch of class. I started in the fall by covering the crabgrass with cardboard and then tossing on many layers of mulch. Into the mulch went some native plants found on our nearby hills, a nettle cutting from friends, and a few medicinal starts from our local nursery. Horehound and sages, fennel and mint, lemon balm, mullein and thyme, verbenas and yarrow, and wild onion and red clover all grow at our house now. They know just what to do, rarely need watering, and love to be pruned and pinched for teas.

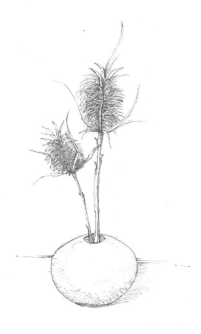

I enjoy the independence of their wild lives, and when they try to take over, I cut them way back and hang the herbs upside down in bunches to dry in my kitchen; the resulting fragrance is quite something. And then, on a rainy winter day, I take down the crackling bunches and strip their leaves into a bowl to replenish my stores of tea. Slowly, I am learning what blends help to calm anxiety; what combination of herbs clears congestion during flu season; what's best for settling an upset stomach. Come on over; I may have exactly what you need.

Wild Foods

My friends Anne Hudes and Steve Ajay are "hunter-gatherers" in our hills. During the rains they hunt out mushrooms and fiddlehead ferns, and in early spring they make salads of the tender greens they find growing everywhere. I am reminded of the most romantic meal I've ever eaten, of mussels plucked from sea rocks, flavored by wild fennel and wine and a crusty loaf of French bread on a faraway beach with a new love, long ago and far away. Mmm.

Food and Medicine

To American Indians, food and medicine are the same thing. The ancient Greek philosopher Hippocrates said, "Let food be your medicine, and your medicine be your food." Onions, for example, helps the gastrointestinal tract to digest, as well as lowering blood pressure and helping to restore sexual function after illness. Got gas? Heartburn? Eat a chopped onion with bread. Got a bad cough? Try onion and honey.

Beet juice, the naturalist and poet Diane Ackerman[18] tells us in *Dawn Light*, when mixed with sage, can soothe a sore throat; dripped into the ear it will help ringing in the ear; and a poultice of beet leaves held on the brow can calm a headache.

Leafy greens—bitters—are good for the liver and help digestion, my herbalist-gardener friend Kait Singley reminds me. She also tells me about signature plants—plants that are shaped like the human body-parts they can help heal, such as kidney beans for the kidneys and walnuts for the brain.

A simple all-around prescription would be to eat a rainbow diet consisting of foods from the color spectrum—greens and yellows and purples and reds. In *Animal, Vegetable, Miracle,*[19] author Barbara Kingsolver's daughter Camille tells us that yellow, orange, and red vegetables can protect our tissues from cancer; green and yellow veggies inhibit tumor growth and block cholesterol absorption; and blue and purple fruits (including purple potatoes) contain flavonoids and antioxidants. Bright yellow flowers—sunflowers, for example—can literally cheer you up, and then you have nutritious and delicious sunflower seeds to eat. If you want to improve your memory, try chocolate-covered garlic ... Eleanor Roosevelt did!

Rebecca Katz,[20] nutritionist and author of *The Cancer Fighting Kitchen,* lists foods that have particular medical and immune-boosting qualities. I thought I would take a look at the anti-inflammatory foods she recommended and found every one of my favorite foods to be on the list, starting with avocados. Blueberries and strawberries made an appearance, as did almonds, lemons, carrots, eggs, salmon, walnuts, sesame, chickpeas, soybeans, broccoli, Swiss chard, millet, and quinoa. This was good news, and not so hard to remember.

We all know that chicken soup is medicinal; I'm quite sure that is more than an old wives' tale (although I believe those old wives were a lot wiser in the ways of the world than we give them credit for.) Chicken soup has healing magic; I've seen it work again and again, both in the making and in the eating. There is something about the combination of chicken, onions, garlic, celery, carrots, parsley, and parsnip cooking in the kitchen that warms the heart, and thus the immune system. In the Southwest, add some green chile! It's in the vitamins and minerals, in the rich, hot broth, in the loving hands preparing it, and in the aromas that pervade the house all day long. Add a little more garlic now, maybe some extra parsley right before serving. Enjoy!

Food Taboos

My friend Song Ping, who came from Peking to study Chemistry in California with my husband one year, once made a remark that put food into perspective for me. We were eating lunch together and talking about eating, as people often do around the table, and she said: "What's all this 'on a diet' in America? Don't eat meat, don't eat sugar. In China, if you have good food, you *eat!*"

In India, the Hindus we lived among were vegetarians, and the Muslims would not eat pork. Bengalis were partial to fish; Orthodox Jews eat neither pork nor shellfish and do not mix meat with milk; the French consider rutabagas horse food; on Crete people mostly avoid fish from the sea surrounding their island. When I serve dinner to friends, I have to make sure I include one dish without meat and one without dairy; no wheat for the gluten-free folks and only honey for the nonsugar folks …

The Art of Being an Omnivore

By nature, I myself am an unrepentant omnivore. I wasn't always, though. At the age of 14, I became a vegetarian—a vegan, actually, although I doubt that the word vegan existed at the time—because I loved animals and wanted to keep Kosher and become pure enough to find God. It was my own private quest, and I didn't tell my friends about it, just my parents. Amazingly, they supported me, probably assuming I would give it up in a few days. But I ended up being disciplined about my diet for almost three years, until one day when I stopped cold turkey, so to speak.

It happened at music camp, where we kids practiced, rehearsed, and performed day and night, eating three huge meals a day that were high in calories, to keep our energy up. At most meals, I carefully picked out the meat and cheese and eggs, avoided the ice cream for dessert, and drank what we called "bug juice" instead of milk. Sometimes, though, the dish was scrambled eggs laced with hamburger and cheese, and when that happened, I lived on bug juice.

I can smile now at the memory, but I scared my flute teacher silly one afternoon when, at my lesson I blew into my flute and fainted dead away at his feet. When I came to, he got the story out of me, then marched me down to the kitchen, got the leftover casserole out of the big fridge, and made me eat it. While I ate—rather famished by that time—he talked to me about true spirituality and the power of music, and how anything that got in the way of making beautiful music was the opposite of what God wanted. I remember him fixing me with soulful eyes to make sure he had made an impression. Then we walked back to his room for my lesson.

I have never looked back. Like Song Ping, I am grateful for the abundance available to me, and I tend to enjoy good food wherever I find it. In fact, I even like *bad* food from time to time, just to keep up with things. So about once a year, we make our way to a hamburger joint for greasy hamburgers with fries, and, well, while I'm in confessional mood, chocolate frosted cupcakes and crinkled potato chips are my junk foods of choice. Why not?

Urban Gardens

I first met Christopher Shein[21] when I took his permaculture class at a local community college, and I have followed his guidance and inspiration ever since. He grew up in suburban Ann Arbor, Michigan, where his mother had a small backyard vegetable garden and a plot in a community garden. In his ordinary-sized backyard, Christopher has created an oasis where he grows an astonishing array of food. He teaches apprentices—volunteers, students, and neighbors—who want to learn what he knows.

His plot is about 50 feet by 75 feet and holds eight raised beds and a few wine barrels verdant with food-bearing plants. His garden, just three years old at this writing, already has 16 bearing fruit trees, perennial greens and herbs, edible vines, swales dug to catch seasonal rains, a one-room strawbale shed, and a small flock of 10 egg-laying chickens. He is raising 25 chicks and four ducklings. Honeybees are arriving this spring from a local honey co-op. He raises enough food to partially feed his own family, not to mention the rest of us who show up to give a hand. He is about to put in a gate to provide access to his neighbor's yard so that both can share in his garden's bounty and Christopher can help with his neighbor's vegetable and fruit garden.

Everything you want to eat is there, along with several things you have never tasted before: many varieties of potatoes and tubers, every variety of greens and beans, tomatoes for slicing and canning, peppers hot and sweet, squashes and brassicas, blueberries and grapes, even tree tomatoes.

Christopher Shein's Permaculture Institute of the East Bay (PIE) is a demonstration and teaching garden that shows what most of us can do with even a little bit of land in the city. Christopher finds that the garden draws generosity like a magnet: people come and volunteer to work, offer seeds and seedlings, mulch, advice, and kitchen scraps for the chickens. As a result, he is able to be generous in return, exporting nutrients to other gardens from his well-mulched beds and chicken runs. His garden is a little paradise in the middle of the city, surrounded by a living bamboo fence that, incidentally, provides bamboo for building projects.

In the center of the garden is an outdoor "room," where vines climb and pumpkins, beans, and grapes hang in season. They create a space of dappled shade, where garden-ers gather for lunch and can pick snacks of grapes and sweet beans from the walls. Christopher is indeed a magician, but he claims that growing food right where you live is what people have always done—he is just bringing back an old custom. That is what our neighbors, Mr. and Mrs. Woiznich, tried to tell my own family those many years ago, had we the ears to hear and the eyes to see.

Chickens

My son Ethan and his wife Anne are home-schooling their children Rob and Eliza-beth in Madison, Wisconsin, and gardening is part of their curriculum. A few years ago, they constructed a chicken coop in their backyard, and everyone worked on it. They brought four newly hatched, fluffy chicks home, and when the chicks were big enough, moved them from the dining room out to the coop in the garden. (The one that turned out to be a rooster has since found a new home in the country.)

In the course of raising the chickens, the children have learned about biology, chem-istry, math, spelling, history, and art, not to mention being in relationship with animal beings. They are responsible for keeping their chickens housed and fed, and for bringing in the eggs. The results are happy family, happy chickens, and delicious eggs.

My friend Judi Petry, who gave up being a Boston surgeon for a more contemplative life in the country, waxes poetic about her gorgeous chickens. I never knew they came in so many shapes and colors! Her flock is larger than Ethan's, but the idea is the same. She wrote me paeans of praise about her "girls," which I will quote here so that you can catch some of her enthusiasm:

> *At about 6–8 months, they lay their first egg, a small thing usually with streaks of blood on the shell suggesting that it is a less than comfortable event. It is so rewarding to come out in the morning to find that first precious reward from the flock, that I usually can't eat it for a day or two. I admire the shape, the color—anything from white to brown to blue-green or pink, and make a ceremony of the first cracking of the first egg shell. The brilliant orange yolk is so different from the pale barely yellow yolks one gets from the grocery that it seems an entirely different food. The white is so fresh it stands on its own, sometimes slithering away from the yolk and asking to be noticed for its own accomplishment.*

And the taste, oh, the taste. It is indeed an epicurean gift of Mother Na-
ture. Each hen lays an egg everyday or every other day while at their peak
of production during their second year of life, and during the non–winter
months. They slow down in the winter, sadly, though it is hard to blame them
for taking a rest …

Stacked Functions

For Chris Shein, keeping chickens is a perfect example of "stacked functions," a permaculture term referring to the fact that everything in the garden should perform
several tasks at once. By where you locate a plant, what companion plants are sited
near it, how their leafing and watering cycles complement each other, and so on, many
functions may be addressed simultaneously. As the permaculturalist Toby Hemenway
puts it, "Nature can do a thousand things at once." And therefore, so should everything in our gardens.

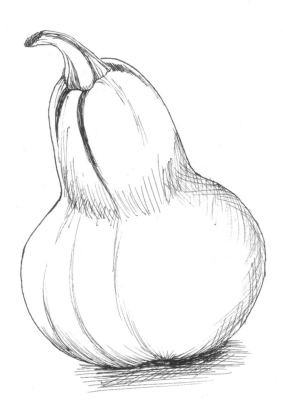

Chickens gobble up weeds and bugs, poop out the most fertile manure there is, burble and cluck satisfyingly, are fascinating to watch, teach kids, are affectionate pets, and only lastly, provide eggs and meat. Some gardeners construct "chicken tractors." These are wicker cages on wheels, like tiny corrals, in which a few chickens can be placed, then transported to the part of the garden that needs weeding or where the slugs tend to hang out. They are covered with their tractor and left there for a day or so of happy pecking, then when they are ready to be moved, that plot will be free of weeds and pests and well fertilized. *Voila!*

I cannot resist mentioning a pair of farmers I know who do this on a larger scale with an old flatbed truck they call a "R-egg-reational Vehicle." Fitted out as a great big chicken coop on wheels, with a ramp and latched windows for fetching the eggs, the truck moves into a field after it is harvested, and the chickens are let out to range. They pick and peck the field free of weed seeds, pests, and stunted plants, liberally fertilizing it with poop.

My favorite example of stacked functions is at the Food For Thought Garden,[22] a suburban garden surrounding the Sonoma County AIDS Food Bank in Northern California. Doug Gosling, head gardener at the Occidental Arts and Ecology Center, and his gardening partner Rachel Gardner have created the most ingenious urban garden I have ever seen, which serves more purposes than I can name.

In a very small space, this garden provides not only an array of fresh vegetables and fruits for the food bank but also a place of healing, where clients can come for quiet reflection or work in the garden for "horticultural therapy." Gourds hang from arbors and trellises, and curved benches surround a small pond shaded by flowering vines. People can sit and talk, eat some lunch, or just stare at the water.

Once a year, the food bank hosts Calabash!, a fundraising event for the Food Bank drawing on the talents of local artists. When the gourds are ready for harvest, artists are invited to come to the garden to choose one from which to create a work of art. And such art! The inventiveness is breathtaking, and as the years go by, the artworks become more fabulously brilliant.

All these pieces are then auctioned off on the day of Calabash! It is like going to the most exciting art gallery you have ever seen—and everyone benefits. All day we stroll the gardens to live music of gourd instruments from Africa, the Middle East, and the Balkans, and eat delicacies prepared from the garden. We bid on our favorite art pieces, meet old friends and new, and learn about what's been going on at the center. There is laughter; there are tears. Doug and Rachel greet us all, smile a lot, and seem happy to pass along their wisdom about simple ways of making a worm bin, or training cherry tomatoes to grow along a fenceline, or planting vines in a small space. It is gardening as art, as healing, and as providing food for every part of ourselves. May they all thrive.

Simplicity

One of the things about permaculture gardening that pleases me so much is its simplicity. Things fit together naturally; words like "getting rid of," "battling," "poisoning," "backbreaking" do not even enter the vocabulary. Your job in the garden is to create the healthy conditions of soil with whatever resources you have available, then let Nature do the rest. It is important to trust that Nature knows how, and to be patient. Henry David Thoreau would approve, I think. "Simplify! Simplify!" he cautioned from his cabin in the woods by Walden Pond.

In fact, one of the most memorable meals I have ever eaten was not in a fancy restaurant but in an isolated hamlet in the Knockmealdown Mountains of Ireland, one cold morning in March while the blacksmith repaired the broken axel on my husband's bike. We had been coasting down the mountain the night before, me at full throttle and my new husband Herb hanging onto the brakes, when his axel had snapped. He'd had to walk his bike all the way down to the valley, where we were stranded in a tiny village of about a dozen souls, one hardscrabble farm, and a handful of sheep and chickens. Two strapping Americans coming into their lives and needing their help had never happened before.

Our visit coincided with the "hungry month," when spring is about to come but the larder is bare, but we were taken in by the blacksmith's wife and offered a bed in the barn. In the morning, God bless them forever, they shared with us their breakfast—a meal I will never forget. The hens had produced four eggs, which she boiled up, a few stalks of rhubarb had been cooked to a tart mash and the daily soda bread was hot from the oven. That was it.

I have tried many times but have never been able to reproduce that breakfast: the creamy richness of those fresh eggs coupled with the sour tang of the rhubarb and the solid bready-ness of the hot loaf. My attempts, of course, lacked the hard frost on the ground, the hint of spring on the air, the adventure of a newly married couple on bikes in the Irish countryside, and the remarkable kindness of strangers. But it was that experience that turned me into a bread baker.

Breads

For all the years our children were growing up we baked our own bread. At first I made soda breads, like the blacksmith's wife, but then I experimented with yeast and assorted grains, playing around with softness and crunch, color and taste. During those years, cooking for our growing family of five was one of the few artistic outlets I had time for, so admittedly, I played it to the hilt.

I always made a dozen loaves at a time, shared the first one, with butter straight from the oven with whoever happened to be around, then sent a hot loaf over to my neighbor Meg (of the neat pickles) in exchange for greens from their garden. My favorite part of the weekly ritual of bread-baking, though, was the lump of dough set aside for pizzas and inventive stuffed delicacies. Every culture in the world has a way of wrapping minced food in dough, serving it as dumplings, turnovers, ravioli, tamales, piroshki, samosas ... I've tried them all.

Starting with pinches of bread dough, I would roll the dough out thin, allow it to rise in a warm oven, then pile on whatever happened to be leftover in the fridge at the moment. A bit of tomato sauce and cheese on flattened dough, and it was Italian pizza; stir-fry vegetables with plum sauce wrapped up in dough became a sort of Chinese *bao*. With the dough rolled over and pinched into a pocket stuffed with bits of hamburger, onion, and potatoes, it was a British pasty; with sautéed onions and spiced mashed potatoes rolled up together, it morphed into a Jewish knish.

The variations are infinite. In our family we called these meals "the first in the history of the world," and as no recipes existed, they were also "the last in the history of the world." They are the last word in nutritious, inexpensive meals and can be as varied as your imagination and your leftovers.

My daughter reminds me about the birthday parties we used to have at our house in which each child was given a ball of dough and a rolling pin and a choice of every kind of topping imaginable for personalized pizzas. Great hilarity ensued, of course, and the cleanup job was considerable, but those pizzas were memorable.

Cooking

"Food," writes Barbara Kingsolver in *Animal, Vegetable, Miracle*, "is not a product but a process, and it never sleeps." I feel that way about cooking. The leftovers of every meal suggest the next meal to come, and although I love cooking with abundant and fresh food, I enjoy cooking most when my larder is relatively bare. I have to be cunning and inventive to come up with a dinner that everybody will like, and it brings out my taste for a challenge.

For example, the days after the big Thanksgiving dinner are my favorite times, when I have to come up with casseroles, sandwiches, or a soup from the turkey carcass and leftover vegetables. That's when I feel my way along to make a soup using thyme, marjoram, and garlic, a few stalks of celery, maybe a dash of fresh lemon from the garden and strong sherry right before serving. For my money, that's when the big turkey starts to make sense.

For those of us who can't stand to cook, I'd suggest that it is just as easy to pop a sweet potato into the microwave and slather it with butter and sesame seeds as it is put in a packaged, prepared meal. Particularly as all that plastic packaging most likely ends up in one of the gyres of garbage now swirling in the middle of our oceans, threatening all of ocean life. It is as easy to steam fresh broccoli or cauliflower as it is to put packaged frozen peas and carrots into boiling water. For those of us who have forgotten how to cook—or never learned in the first place because our mothers or fathers didn't cook—this is the time to learn.

Valuable Leftovers

A few days after Thanksgiving one year, I stopped at a neighbor's house for something, and there on her kitchen table was the inevitable turkey carcass with about two pounds of meat left on the bone, and a scattering of stuffing and green beans sitting forlornly around it. She gazed at it impatiently and then held it aloft over the garbage can.

"I'm sick of this thing," she sighed, letting it plop unceremoniously into the trash. I almost reached out to catch it, but I think it was at that moment the idea for my food recovery project, Daily Bread, was officially born.

I went home and with my husband calculated that if everyone on our street of about 25 households tossed out their turkeys, each with an average of two pounds of meat still on the bone, then our block alone would be tossing 50 pounds of food into the trash. Multiply that by the whole city, and the number was incalculable. Include the state and the country, and we were talking about tons of waste—all in one day! It would then go into stinking dumps and perhaps out to sea on barges to feed the gulls.

I was sure we could do better than that.

I often wonder how much perfectly good food goes down the drain simply because we don't know what to do with leftovers. For many of us, fresh food is available every day in stores—we've been lucky—but that is not always the case for everyone, and it may change for all of us. If and when that happens, we would do well to know how to improvise with what we've got around. Not knowing what to make for dinner probably has less to do with the resources available than it does with a failure of imagination.

Let's start with this handful of turkey and see how many gourmet dishes we might make from it. I will stick to ideas that require minimal preparation time. These are not recipes so much as a basic guide for leftovers of all kinds.

SOUPS. In a large pot, add whole turkey carcass as is, water to cover and throw in vegetables—even leftover salad. Add herbs to taste, salt and pepper. Simmer all day. To make it fancy, blend all ingredients in a blender before serving and add cream.

STEWS AND CASSEROLES. Sauté onions and garlic, add celery, carrots, and whatever other vegetables you have around, add turkey and season with herbs and greens. To make it sweet and sour, add raisins, apples, and lemon. To make it Asian-tasting, add soy sauce and coriander leaves. Serve over grains or pasta.

STIR-FRY. Slice vegetables and turkey into thin strips. Heat oil in wok or frying pan, toss in and cook quickly. Stir-fry it. Serve over rice.

FRITTERS. Dice turkey pieces, thinly slice vegetables that crunch (onions, cabbage, peppers), mix them together with two eggs and a cup of flour until it forms a chunky paste. Drop spoonfuls into oil in a very hot skillet. Serve the fritters with interesting toppings, such as toasted sesame seeds, soy sauce, plum sauce, or applesauce.

COLD SALAD. Combine diced turkey with mayonnaise, boiled potatoes, mustard, chopped onion, parsley, chopped celery. Serve the way you would serve tuna salad.

Use these as seed ideas. I have not indicated amounts because I'm not very good at following recipes, but a good eye and common sense is really all you need. The possibilities are infinite. For example, think chili beans and turkey; open-face hot sandwiches; filling for tacos, burritos, and stuffed pita bread; pot pies; stuffed peppers; meatballs; pizza...

If you are ever tempted to toss that old turkey out, think again. Or call Daily Bread.

Tuesday Soup

Most every cuisine in the world has a version of the Danish Tuesday Soup, in which the week's leftovers are tossed into the same pot, water is added, and the whole stew is cooked into a soup. It is invariably delicious, never the same twice, and always nutritious. In our family we called it "the Mendocino Mish-mash" in honor of the week we spent in a rented place on the Mendocino coast where we had to prepare all our meals in the cottage's single cooking pot. My grown children, I have noted with pride, are still making variations on those mish-mash meals in their own kitchens.

Things are serious in the world now, and being self-reliant and creative may be important survival techniques; the kitchen is probably an excellent place to begin. As the saying goes, "If the world hands you lemons, make lemonade." If the eggs crack when you drop the grocery bag, scramble them fast! If you have only a can of tuna fish and some stale bread in the cupboard, make a tuna-fish casserole with breadcrumbs, and find a way to make it delicious. Be flexible. Get inventive. Just don't give up.

About two years after our stay in China, I learned this the hard way. We received a surprise phone call from one of my students from Fudan University who had made it out to San Francisco with a delegation of young journalists. Could he come to see us?

"Of course!" we replied, delighted to reconnect with him, and thinking we might bring up some questions it would have been impolite (and impolitic) to ask while we were there. "Come for dinner."

"May I bring two or three of my classmates?"

"Of course!" So I cooked up a stir-fry of broccoli, onions, garlic, and chicken, filled a pot of rice for about 10 people, and sent the children out for a gallon of ice cream. When he showed up, it was not with two or three, but with the whole delegation of 20 students!

I went totally still, as I tend to do when in shock, and for five minutes could not speak. Then I took a deep breath and moved into action. Out the back door went my daughter to gather up every vegetable the neighbors had on hand; and both sons joined the students in the living room to keep everyone entertained, while Herb ran to the liquor store on the corner to buy up all the ice cream and cookies they had in stock. Pots of rice were set boiling on neighbors' stoves, and the stir-fry grew exponentially as cabbages and carrots, potatoes and bell peppers came in through the back door, were cut up on the chopping block, then put into three woks.

The crowd in front knew nothing of the frenzied scene in the kitchen, but in under an hour my daughter and I had dinner ready for 25, and all our neighbors were peering out their windows at the extravaganza next door. When the evening was over, the dinner party was deemed a success, although in that bedlam there was no way we could talk with our friend about the discreet matters we were hoping to broach. Which, it occurred to us later, might not have been a complete coincidence.

Play With Your Food

For those of us who enjoy cooking, it's fun to sometimes play with our food. Adrienne Robinson, one of the most creative people I have ever known, and a friend and collaborator for over three decades, once gave our family a unique Christmas present: a marionette puppet of a ballerina, complete with dancing arms and legs, all made out of bread. As a multimedia sculptor, she uses bread dough as one of her media. I love watching her knead that dough until it is smooth and springy, shaping and rolling bits of it until, out of her clever hands come big-bosomed mermaids, lions lying down with lambs, dragons and lovers, and guys riding bicycles! She knows just how each shape will rise in the baking, and scales her creatures accordingly. I am always reminded of the Creator creating the world when I watch her sculpt in bread, and although she insists we eat the sculptures after they have been admired, I always want to hang them on my wall. She teaches her techniques to children and adults, and even if sculpting is not your particular gift, you'll find there is something deeply satisfying about having fragrant, elastic dough in your hands to shape however you wish.

She plays with vegetables as well, and in her hands a bell pepper, two bananas, three potatoes, and a handful of radishes might become a wild garden or a scene from The Creation. Her masterpiece of all time was, in my eyes, the portrait she created of her brother from a lobster claw, which actually looked like him!

We may not all be as whimsical or adept as Adrienne, but food fun abounds in more ordinary ways as well. Jokes may be sent to school with the children in their lunchboxes: carrots carved into weird shapes, layered sandwiches that are striped when bitten into. Cookies may carry messages or be dropped mischievously into coat pockets.

My niece Cristie writes:

> *Sometimes when I prepare my husband's meal—whether it's at home*
> *for dinner or a packed lunch—I sneak in a chocolate chip or prune in a most*
> *unexpected place: in a salad, in between the layers of a sandwich, under a fish*
> *filet, in the middle of his corn muffin. Once he unwrapped his sandwich that*
> *I had taken a bite out of AND put a prune in; his whole office was laughing.*

KISS THE COOK reads a poster created by the calligrapher Georgianna Greenwood.[23] She told me that it was originally printed on an apron in the 1970s, Today, the poster of the slogan is something of a national icon. It hangs in homes and restaurants all across the country and even appeared on a kitchen wall in a film. It's a good idea to remember to kiss the cook...

For those who enjoy going to great lengths to be playful, there's always the Fresh Vegetable Orchestra[24] from Vienna, a real orchestra in which musicians play concerts all over the world using vegetables as instruments. They play leek violins, hollowed out carrot and daikon radish flutes, cucumber and bell-pepper horns, pumpkins drums and eggplant-half clackers, cabbage and dried bean percussions. Their music is real, beautiful and, of course, hilarious. It takes knowing how to shop, how to carve vegetables, and last but not least, knowing how to make the music.

Do you remember the old folktale "Stone Soup?" It's Russian, I think. A starving soldier comes into a village in the middle of winter, and people shut their doors to him. He begins gathering stones in the village square, and when they ask what he is doing he says he will make a magical stone soup that will feed everyone in the village. So they fetch him a huge pot, build a fire, and wait to be shown this miracle.

"Yumm," he says, gathering stones and placing them carefully in the pot, "this is going to be great soup, but with a few onions it could be really marvelous." Someone runs off to bring him onions. He sniffs the heating onion broth and says, "With a couple of carrots, maybe a dozen, it will taste even sweeter." And then it is potatoes and beans and turnips and meat, each of which is brought by someone in the village to add to the pot until the soup is bubbling and sending up delicious wafts of steam, making everyone hungry for the best soup they have ever smelled. Gallantly, he shares his stone soup with everyone in the village, until, like people everywhere after a satisfying meal, everyone is laughing and dancing with delight. They've had the best soup in the world, and it was only made from stones! A miracle.

I get similar sensuous satisfaction from the whole process of getting food onto the table. I am as nourished by the colors and design of food—slice into a beet, a lemon, an apple, and what do you see?—as I am by what it tastes like. A salad made from bright green arugula, crisp red peppers, and thin slices of white daikon radish is a visual as well as a culinary feast. Close your eyes and recall the mouth-watering aroma that pervades the whole house when a chicken, basted with lemon juice and rosemary, is roasting in the oven—the crackling skin sizzling with a hint of lemon zest and garlic, the rich spice of bread stuffing laced with sage and onions, crisping on top of lemony gravy...

Anne Hudes puts quinces into a warm oven overnight, so that the house will smell of baking quince when everyone wakes up in the morning. Sweet potatoes give off their spicy fragrance for days and, of course, baking bread is the scent of heaven.

Cooking satisfies some deep hunger for beauty and plentitude in me, and I step back to admire the play of soft mozzarella cheese and ripe, juicy tomatoes taking shape on my work table. I add to it thin slices of red onion, leaves of green basil fresh from the garden, then I trickle on olive oil followed by red-wine vinegar. A dash of salt, some pepper, and it's ready. Hungry?

Eating

And now, at last, it is time for supper. Perhaps you are eating alone, your plate filled with your favorite foods; perhaps it is a candlelight dinner for two, or the gathering of the clan at the end of the day to share a pot of soup and stories. However you do it, it's a time for replenishment, tasting, and satisfying your body and soul.

I was once taught a mindfulness practice that consisted of the slow eating of a single raisin. We had to do nothing but eat that raisin, small bite by small bite, tasting it thoroughly, and swallowing before we raised it back to our mouths for the next bite. It was a revelation, something of a miniature orgy. Try it.

I often remember that raisin while I am eating and try to eat slowly and mindfully, not for any particular spiritual purpose but just because food tastes better that way. Anyhow, why go to all that trouble to cook if you're not going to relish it?

Take stock. Enjoy. Digest. Be grateful. Be nourished.

Stacked functions … of course.

Bon appétit.

> *Begin as creation, become a creator. Never wait at a barrier*
> *In this kitchen stocked with fresh food,*
> *why sit content with a cup of warm water?*
>
> — RUMI

ADDITIONAL INSPIRATIONS

Adrienne's Bread Sculpture Recipe

INGREDIENTS
- 8 cups flour
- ½ cup oil
- 1 cup sugar
- 1 tsp salt
- 2 cups warm water
- 2 tbs yeast
- 2 eggs (save 1 white)

INSTRUCTIONS

Dissolve yeast in small amount of warm water. Add salt, oil, flour, sugar, and eggs. Mix until all in one lump. Turn out on board and knead until it feels smooth and silky and springy. Put dough into oiled bowl, turn once, and cover with damp towel and let rise till double (2–4 hours).

When making sculptures build directly on oiled cookie sheets, as sculptures are almost impossible to move once shaped. Use your hands as if they were a rolling pin. Do not stretch or pull dough. Add pieces onto each other. If they are difficult to attach, a tiny dap of water will stick them together. Use your imagination. You can make flowers, storybook characters, buildings, monsters, and sport and super heroes. Leave an inch or two between finished sculptures as they almost double in size and will stick together if too close.

Bake at 350 degrees for 20–45 minutes, depending on size, or until golden brown. Whip remaining egg white and brush onto sculpture after baking.

Magic With Cucumbers

This remarkable list of cucumber attributes arrived one day from I know not where. I offer it just as received.

- **Cucumbers contain most of the vitamins you need every day.** Just one cucumber contains vitamin B1, vitamin B2, vitamin B3, vitamin B5, vitamin

B6, folic acid, vitamin C, calcium, iron, magnesium, phosphorus, potassium, and zinc.

- **Feeling tired in the afternoon? Put down the caffeinated soda and pick up a cucumber.** As mentioned above, cucumbers are a good source of B vitamins and carbohydrates that can provide that quick pickmeup that can last for hours.

- **Tired of your bathroom mirror fogging up after a shower?** Try rubbing a cucumber slice along the mirror: it will eliminate the fog and provide a soothing, spalike fragrance.

- **Are grubs and slugs ruining your planting beds?** Place a few slices in a small pie tin and your garden will be free of pests all season long. The chemicals in the cucumber react with the aluminum to give off a scent undetectable to humans but drive garden pests crazy and make them flee the area.

- **Looking for a fast and easy way to remove cellulite before going out or to the pool?** Try rubbing a slice or two of cucumbers along your problem area for a few minutes. The phytochemicals in the cucumber cause the collagen in your skin to tighten, firming up the outer layer, and reducing the visibility of cellulite. Works great on wrinkles, too!

- **Want to avoid a hangover or terrible headache?** Eat a few cucumber slices before going to bed and wake up refreshed and headache free. Cucumbers contain enough sugar, B vitamins, and electrolytes to replenish essential nutrients the body has lost, keeping everything in equilibrium, and avoiding both a hangover and headache!

- **Looking to fight off that afternoon or evening snacking binge?** Cucumbers have been used for centuries and often by European trappers, traders, and explorers for quick meals to thwart off starvation.

- **Have an important meeting or job interview and you realize that you don't have enough time to polish your shoes?** Rub a freshly cut cucumber over the shoe. Its chemicals will provide a quick and durable shine that not only looks great but also repels water.

- **Need to fix a squeaky hinge?** Take a cucumber slice and rub it along the problematic hinge, and *voila,* the squeak is gone!

- **Stressed out and don't have time for a massage, facial, or visit to the spa?**
- Cut up an entire cucumber and place it in a boiling pot of water. The chemicals and nutrients from the cucumber with react with the boiling water and are released in the steam, creating a soothing, relaxing aroma that has been shown the reduce stress in new mothers and college students during final exams.

- **Just finished a business lunch and realize you don't have gum or mints?**
- Take a slice of cucumber and press it to the roof of your mouth with your tongue for 30 seconds to eliminate bad breath. The phytochemcials will kill the bacteria in your mouth responsible for causing bad breath.
- **Looking for a "green" way to clean your taps, sinks or stainless steel?**
- Take a slice of cucumber and rub it on the surface you want to clean; not only will it remove years of tarnish and bring back the shine but it won't leave streaks and won't harm you fingers or fingernails while you clean.
- **Using a pen and made a mistake?** Take the outside of the cucumber and slowly use it to erase the pen writing. Also works great on crayons and markers that the kids have used to decorate the walls!

The Edible Schoolyard (ESY), a program of the Chez Panisse Foundation, is a one-acre organic garden and kitchen classroom for urban public school students at Martin Luther King, Jr. Middle School in Berkeley, California, where classroom teachers and gardening teachers integrate food systems concepts into the core curriculum. Students' hands-on experience in the kitchen and garden fosters a deeper appreciation of how the natural world sustains us and promotes the environmental and social well-being of our community. For more information, visit www.edibleschoolyard.org

Jamie's Food Revolution, the brainchild of British celebrity chef Jamie Oliver, started out as a unique televised community program to improve school lunches in the United Kingdom and attracted the support of the British government. A similar program was successfully begun in Huntingdon, West Virginia, in the United States, and was the subject of an ABC television show called *Jamie's Food Revolution* in 2010. Oliver is devoted to saving our health by changing the way we eat. For more information visit www.jamieoliver.com

Ecology Centers provide environmental education and local stewardship through information, books, and staff available to help with a wide range of issues. Check around for ecology centers in your area. For more information, visit www.ecologycenter.org/bfm

Biodynamic Farming is a method of organic farming that treats farms as unified and individual organisms. It emphasizes balancing the holistic development and inter-relationship of the soil, plants, animals as a self-nourishing system without external inputs insofar as this is possible, given the loss of nutrients due to the export of food. Regarded by some as the first modern ecological farming system and one of the most sustainable, biodynamic farming has much in common with other organic approaches, such as emphasizing the use of manures and composts and excluding the use of artificial chemicals on soil and plants. Methods unique to the biodynamic approach include the use of fermented herbal and mineral preparations as compost additives and field sprays and the use of an astronomical sowing and planting calendar. Biodynamics originated out of the work of Rudolf Steiner, the founder of the spiritual philosophy anthroposophy. For more information, visit *www.biodynamics.com*

ENDNOTES

1.   **Michael Pollan** has been writing books and articles for the last 20 years about the places where the human and natural worlds intersect: food, agriculture, gardens, drugs, and architecture. For more information, visit *www.michaelpollan. com*

2.   **Wendy Johnson** is a Buddhist meditation teacher and organic gardening mentor in the San Francisco Bay Area. For more information, visit *www.gardeningat-thedragonsgate.com/about_author_illustrator.html*

3.   **Farmers Markets** are an integral part of the urban/farm linkage and have continued to rise in popularity, mostly due to the growing consumer interest in obtaining fresh products directly from the farm. Direct marketing of farm products through farmers markets continues to be an important sales outlet for agricultural producers nationwide. For more information about farmers markets in your area, visit *www.ams.usda.gov* in the United States, or *http://www.farmersmarkets.net* in the United Kingdom.

4.   **Community Supported Agriculture (CSA)** is a community of individuals who pledge support to a farmer at the beginning of the growing season. Members pay in advance the anticipated costs of the farm operation and farmer's salary, and in return, receive weekly delivery of the produce throughout the growing season. They may help with farmwork and harvesting. By this collaboration, growers and customers benefit. So does the farm! For more information, visit *http://www.nal. usda.gov/afsic/pubs/csa/csa.shtml* or *www.localharvest.org*

5.   **Full Belly Farm** has used organic practices since 1985 and produces an amazing diversity of vegetables, herbs, nuts, flowers, and fruits year round as a Community Supported Agricultural project. Organic wool and organic wines also available. For more information, visit *www.fullbellyfarm.com*

6.   **Daily Bread** is a grassroots operation that for 26 years has picked up surplus food from food businesses and brings the food directly to local free-food kitchens, pantries, and shelters. All food runners and coordinators are volunteers, and the organization operates with virtually no budget. For more information, visit *www.healingimprovisations.net/social/dailybread*

7.   The **locavore movement** in the United States and elsewhere developed out of a growing interest in locally based sustainability and eco-consciousness. Local foods may be grown in home gardens or grown by local commercial groups

interested in keeping the environment as clean as possible and selling food close to where it is grown. Those in the movement generally seek to lower their carbon footprint, keeping "food miles" and fossil fuels for the transport of food to a minimum. For more information, visit www.locavores.com and *www.tigersand-strawberries.com/category/the-locavores-bookshelf*

8.   **Slow Food** is a nonprofit, ecogastronomic, member-supported organization that was founded in 1989 to counteract fast food and fast life, the disappearance of local food traditions, and people's dwindling interest in the food they eat, where it comes from, how it tastes, and how our food choices affect the rest of the world. For more information, visit *www.slowfood.com*

9.   **Polyface Farm and Metropolitan Buying Clubs** offer ways of buying your meat and dairy groceries directly from farmers, the best way to keep track of your impact both on the environment and on your body. Large-scale meat and dairy operations (CAFOs) often raise a number of concerns, including waste runoff into local water supplies, use of hormones and antibiotics, and crowded animal living conditions. A local meat and dairy farmer can supply you with meat and dairy from healthy and humanely raised animals. For more information, visit *http://www.polyfacefarms.com/taste.aspx*

10. **The White House Organic Farm Project** is an organic kitchen garden at the White House started by First Lady Michelle Obama with the help of fifth-graders from a local public school. For more information, visit: *www.thewhofarm.org*

11. **Wendell Berry** is a poet, man of letters, and farmer living in Kentucky who disapproves of computer technology, and thus has no website. For more information about him, try Googling Wendell Berry to find his books and essays.

12. **Indoor Gardening** is about growing small edible plants like herbs and greens on indoor windowsills. For more information, visit *www.cooks garden.com*

13. **Richard Register** is one of the world's great theorists and authors in ecological city design and planning. He is president of Ecocity Builders, a nonprofit organization dedicated to reshaping cities, towns, and villages for long-term health of human and natural systems. The organization's goals include returning healthy biodiversity to the heart of our cities, agriculture to gardens and streets, and convenience and pleasure to walking, bicycling, and public transit. The organization visualizes a future in which waterways in neighborhood environments and prosperous downtown centers are opened for curious children, fish, frogs, and dragonflies. It works to build thriving neighborhood centers while reversing sprawl development. For more information, visit *www.ecocitybuilders.org*

14. Permaculture is an approach to designing human settlements and agricultural systems that mimics the relationships found in natural ecologies. Permaculture involves sustainable land-use design and is based on ecological and biological principles, often using patterns that occur in Nature for maximum effect and minimum work. It aims to create stable, productive systems that provide for human needs, harmoniously integrating the land with its inhabitants, all elements in a system viewed in relationship to other elements, where the outputs of one element become the inputs of another. These principles can be applied to any environment, at any scale, from dense urban settlements to individual homes, from farms to entire regions.
For more information, visit *www.permaculture.org*

15. **Toby Hemenway** is the author of the first major North American book on permaculture, Gaia's Garden: A Guide to Home-Scale Permaculture (Chelsea Green 2001). His website includes information on permaculture workshops and courses, principles of permaculture, an extensive reading list, articles, and links. For more information, visit *www.patternliteracy.com*

16. **John Todd, Ecological Designer** is an internationally recognized inventor and a pioneer in the design and construction of ecological wastewater treatment systems, offering a cost-effective, renewable solutions to the growing global wastewater crisis. His company has created practical designs in 11 countries on five continents around the world. For more information, visit *www.toddecological.com*

17. **Edward O. Wilson** is a biologist who explores the world of ants and other tiny creatures and writes movingly about the interdependence of all creatures, great and small. He makes a plea that we learn more about our biosphere and build a networked encyclopedia of all the world's knowledge about life. For more information, visit *www.eowilson.org*

18. **Diane Ackerman** is a poet, essayist, naturalist, and teacher who scours the world to see and understand natural patterns in everything, For more information, visit *http://www.dianeackerman.com*

19. **Barbara Kingsolver**, the novelist, has written a memoir about one year of eating solely what could be produced by her family and their local Tennessee community. Entitled *Animal, Vegetable, Miracle* (HarperCollins 2008), the book contains stories, research about food production, and charming essays by Kingsolver's 19-year-old daughter Camille. For more information, visit *www.animalvegetablemiracle.com*

20. **Rebecca Katz** is transforming health through the power of food. She is a chef and nuturitionist who has written about healing diets for cancer patients. For more information, visit *www.rebecccakatz.com*

21. **Christopher Shein and Wildheart Gardens** is garden design that specializes in permaculture designs. He uses local native seed and plants, as well as edibles. Greywater, rainwater, and chickens are another layer in the deepening ecological garden web of life. For more information, visit *www.wildheartgardens.com*

22. **Occidental Arts & Ecology Center (OAEC)** is a nonprofit organizing and education center and organic farm in Northern California. Much of the center's work addresses the challenges of creating democratic communities that are ecologically, economically, and culturally sustainable in an increasingly privatized and corporatized economy and culture. OAEC's programs combine research, demonstration, education, and organizing to develop collaborative, community-based strategies for positive social change and effective environmental stewardship. It is the sponsoring organization for the Food For Thought Gardens at the Sonoma County AIDS Food Bank. For more information, visit *www.oaec.org*. To learn more about Calabash! visit *www.fftfoodbank.org/content/calabash*

23. **Georgianna Greenwood** learned calligraphy from Lloyd J. Reynolds. She has been teaching and practicing calligraphy and related arts in the California Bay Area and elsewhere since 1964. For more information, visit *www.friendsof calligraphy.org*

24. The **Vienna Vegetable Orchestra** performs music solely on instruments made of vegetables. Using carrot flutes, pumpkin basses, leek violins, leek-zucchini-vibrators, cucumberophones, and celery bongos, the orchestra creates its own extraordinary and vegetabile sound universe. The ensemble overcomes preserved and marinated sound conceptions or tirelessly restewed listening habits, putting its focus on expanding the variety of vegetable instruments, developing novel musical ideas, and exploring fresh vegetable "sound gardens." For more information, visit *www.gemueseorchester.org*

CHAPTER THREE

WASTE

Nature assembles and breaks down, dissolves and renews,
using the same molecules over and over. She leaves no
landfills and toxic dumps in her wake. In nature there is no
such thing as waste. Everything is food for something else,
connected in life and death to many other species.

—*TOBY HEMENWAY* [1]

GAIA'S GARDEN, A GUIDE TO HOME-SCALE PERMACULTURE

It was my third pregnancy, and it was going on and on. The due date had passed, and a week later there was still no sign of this baby. The month was May, the roses were blooming, and I was like a beached whale stranded on the beach. I figured I would be pregnant for the rest of my life.

Next door to us lived a retired couple whose hobby was roses. Each day they would pluck the roses just past their first bloom from their many rosebushes and set them in cardboard cartons on the sidewalk for the trash collectors to pick up. Masses of these fragrant blossoms were set out daily, still perfectly intact as far as I could see. Well, I was just sitting around anyway, so why not try out a recipe for rose-petal jam I had found in a Greek cookbook? It was as good a way as any to pass this time of waiting.

You know the outcome: as soon as those millions of rose petals were bubbling on the stove the baby made his insistent appearance, and I had to leave the pot on simmer while we ran off to the hospital to give birth.

My obstetrician was a good friend, and I was allowed to go home a day early so I could get back to the older children, as well as my jam. The new baby's second day of life was spent smelling rose petals as the jam got put up into glass canning jars by everyone in the house, including me.

Our neighbors, of course, received the first jar of rose-petal jam, and ever thereafter referred to me as the "lady who made something out of nothing."

Something Out of Nothing

We all make "something" out of an apparent "nothing" everyday, and it doesn't smell like roses. To mention the unmentionable: we all produce our daily measure of urine and excrement, and most of us do not have any idea where it goes. In the natural world, the waste products of plants and animals cycle back into the soil, providing nutrients for the next generations, available to all of life. Not so for us humans. And therein lies our dilemma: what to do with our wastes?

The children's book *Who Poops?* starts with the line "If you eat, you poop," then each page shows a different animal pooping and the shape of turd it makes. The last page shows a human child sitting on a potty—the only creature *not* to leave its excrement on the ground.

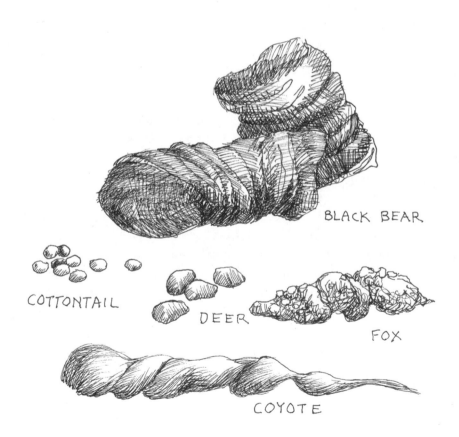

BLACK BEAR

COTTONTAIL

DEER

FOX

COYOTE

Except for breathing, defecating is probably the most intimate exchange we have with the natural world. As we breathe, we and all the other animals release our waste product, carbon dioxide, into the air. It is inhaled by the plant kingdom—used; the plants, in turn, exhale their oxygen, which we animals then breathe in. It is a perfect exchange; everything is needed and nothing is wasted.

Likewise, animals consume plants either directly or through other animals who feed on plants and excrete their own wastes back into the soil. Their poop, in turn, provides the nitrogen and phosphorus the plants need to grow. The liquids soak into the soil, and the solid matter dries, is attacked by flies and fungi and rain, and becomes good, sweet-smelling earth again in short order. It is a closed-loop cycle in which nothing is wasted, everything is transformed and useful and, as permaculture guru Toby Hemenway says, produces no toxic landfills.

And then you get to us humans sitting on that toilet. The closed loop has a loophole, and that's where the trouble begins.

Facts And Figures

- Disease spread by human bodily waste kills more people worldwide than any other single cause of death.
- Two-thirds of the world is without sanitation.
- Most humans spend about three years of their life urinating and defecating.
- A gram of feces contains 10 million viruses, 1 million bacteria, 1,000 parasite cysts, and 100 worm eggs.
- Wastewater practices worldwide discharge 1.46 trillion gallons of polluted discharge—raw untreated sewage—into the nearest bodies of water on a regular basis.
- By 2020, the proportion of crumbling, dangerous sewer pipes in the United Kingdom will be 50 percent.
- To reform sanitation in most countries, entire systems of governance need to be changed.
- In the United States, the average person produces almost five pounds of municipal solid waste *daily*.
- One hundred billion pieces of junk mail are distributed annually in the United States.
- About 400 million used electronic products are thrown away annually.
- Roughly, 5 percent of the world's population lives in the United States but uses 30 percent of the world's resources.

A Brief History of Shit

Much of what I have learned about excrement comes from Rose George's[2] splendid book, *The Big Necessity: The Unmentionable World of Human Waste and Why it Matters*, which is chock full of hard facts on this little-discussed subject. I am hoping that the temptation to pun will not distract my narrative, but I may not be able to hold it in. Please forgive me in advance for my indiscretions.

The word shit comes from a root word in Greek and Latin that means "to divide, or separate." The word waste comes from a Latin root word meaning "uncultivated," so I will use shit to refer to human excrement, as I believe it ought to be cultivated rather than wasted. I am reminded of that scene in one of Dr. Suess's Grinch stories where someone asks if he might go to the "euphemism."

Rose George claims that our shit is "as rich as oil, and probably more useful," but during human history has been an unsolved dilemma that people would rather not talk about. Everywhere, and always, though, the upper classes had options that the lower classes did not, mostly because they had other people deal with their shit, rather than having to do it themselves.

When people lived rurally, in small villages and encampments, shitting happened in specified locations, onto or into the ground. Those in tribal villages by large rivers shat right into the rivers; the local fish benefited, and the river stayed clean. On land, the liquids leached back into the soil, and the solids were covered with earth and allowed to mulch. But as people moved closer together and population centers grew, there was too much of the stuff to contend with. What to do? Well, the upper classes built separate little huts, or deep pits in the ground, or run-off sewers that went "that-a-way"—*away* being the significant word—and the poor continued to shit on the ground. Worldwide, to a great extent, this is still true.

Where I lived in India in the 1960s, the fields and lanes surrounding our rural home were obstacle courses of shitpiles. Even though Gandhi had tried to teach *tatti par mitti*, which means, "please cover your shit with soil," most of the village men simply go out into the field at dawn to do their business, expecting the scavenger pigs to do the job. The women, out of modesty and custom, shit after dark, but that comes with its own dangers, including vulnerability to attack and not seeing where you are stepping. Can you imagine the logistics of squatting in the dark while dealing with five yards of sari cloth?

Results of recent latrine-building efforts in the villages were less than successful, as the brick latrines in some places were better built than the mud houses people were living in. The bush was perfectly adequate for the peoples' needs, so the new latrines often became village temples instead of shit houses.

I worked in the local clinic near Kalianpur, in the Ganges Plain, and during the dry season most people who came into the clinic had skin wounds that had gone septic. A simple cut on the hand could be disastrous because of the polluted dust produced by the 200,000 tons of shit produced in India everyday, which blew everywhere. (The advertising slogan "There is an Air About India" is one you can take literally.) But on the day the monsoons started, we were inundated by people with dysentery of every description, from cholera to amoebaiasis. Waterborne disease vectors were in everything people touched, drank, washed with, and ate.

I was as careful as I could possibly be, but one day I was offered a cup of tea by a fellow worker at the clinic that I felt I couldn't refuse. The result was a case of bacillary dysentery so severe I thought I would never recover. But I learned firsthand what millions of people face as a matter of course, and what children, worldwide and by the millions, die of every year.

Wastewater treatment in India is some version of dumping it into the holy rivers. I still try to comprehend this. My friend Pradip who, as a young chemist, was trying to find ways of cleaning up the Ganges River, was severely beaten one night by religious zealots—because of his work, we believe—and left for dead. He survived, thank God, and has gone on to be one of India's most prominent scientists. And the rivers are still polluted, and still holy.

Shit Happens

When I was a student in France, one of my jobs as a nanny was to empty the children's chamber pots in the morning. This was the 20th century, and the family could afford a servant to do the job—me—but less than 100 years earlier I might have emptied those same chamber pots out the window, crying out *Gardez-l'eau!* ("Watch out for the water!") Ever wonder where the British word *loo* came from? Or why people, men and women, used to all wear high-heeled shoes?

In China, right after the Cultural Revolution, we shat into proper toilets, but their flushes went not to a sewage pipe and then into a sewer that took it all away but right into a barrel beneath the apartment block where we lived. Every evening a "honey-bucket" truck would come by and take our shit and piss away to the fields just past the houses, where much of our food was grown.

One day I took a walk out to the fields, wandering up and down rows of bok choy, all green and thriving, being hand-watered by women with buckets balanced across their shoulders. With long-handled dippers they would patiently fill their dippers from the buckets, and water the roots of each individual plant, and when the buckets were empty, they would walk to the large cesspit at the bottom of each row for a refill.

The cesspits were in various stages of fermentation and, of course, the most fermented were used for the watering. Secretly, I wondered if any of the turds in the fresh pools might be mine.

If you have ever wondered why Chinese cuisine does not include salads, or why you have to heat the oil in the wok until it sizzles right out of the pan, that is why. But it is a system that has worked for 4,000 years and it is the reason why Chinese fields still have healthy soil even after four millennia of intensive agriculture. You just have to know how to do it safely. And Chinese food, as we all know, is superb.

China, I've been told, is "fecal-philiac," or appreciative of excrement, while India is "fecal-phobic," the opposite. In China, the deity of the toilet is a beautiful lady; in India, the deity is the river itself, now deadly.

From the Arctic comes a true story of an elderly man who, as a way of saving his life during a winter storm, defecated and when his shit froze, fashioned it into a blade with the help of some of his spit, with which he killed and flayed one of his dogs. From the dog's ribcage he created a sled, and from its pelt he made a harness for the remaining dog and then, as ethnographer Wade Davis,[3] who tells this story in *The Wayfinders* says, "he disappeared into the darkness." Now *that* is "fecal-phenomenal!"

Humanure

The view from the outdoor privy on a friend's farm faces out over a river valley to misty mountains beyond. I bring my binoculars to watch the birds when I use it. It is a charming little place, decorated like a Victorian dollhouse on stilts, with a sweet wooden toilet seat, pictures on the walls, and an antique coal scuttle to hold sawdust, and sometimes wood ash. (Adding some mushroom spawn might be a good idea here, too.) After each use, the ash or sawdust is tossed into a 55-gallon drum beneath the floor. The only thing the outhouse lacks is a front door; how else could we see the view?

I was told it takes about two years for the hole to fill, then another two years for the contents of the drum to "cook" out in the sun, its metal lid tightly sealed on top. After two years, the new sweet-smelling soil is ready to be spread onto the flowerbeds and orchard (but not the vegetables.) While one drum is mulching a second drum is substituted, and the whole process begins again.

Composting toilet systems are not for everyone, nor is the city the best place to consider having one, but especially for those in the country, or new housing develop-ments, they are a whole new—or rather old—way to go. No more land-destroying septic systems and leach fields. No more breach in the natural loop of land to animal, animal to land. No more excessive use of perfectly clean flushing water.

In one style of composting toilet system, you sit up front to pee where the urine is collected, and scoot to the back of the drum to shit. This requires a bit of agility, but is a great way to strengthen the lower-body muscles. In another style, the scooting is not required, I am told. The urine can be harvested frequently and diluted with water before being used to water the trees, while the dry shit and sawdust breaks down into sweet-smelling compost in short order.

In another, much simpler style of composting, you pee and poop into a small bucket—as you would into a flush toilet—but after each use, the contents get emptied into a special compost bin and covered with straw everyday.

We're trying out everything, it seems, and Christina Bertea, plumber and clean water advocate, claims it is about time. With flush toilets becoming increasingly the rage all around the world, more and more of the world's fresh water supplies are disappearing down the drains.

Wastewater and Sludge

Cleaning up wastewater in our septic water-flush system involves first filtering out the solids, then aerating the remaining water so that oxygen can feed the microorganisms. They, in turn, break down all the organic content still present in the water. The result is water clean enough to flow back into our pipes, our streams, and our oceans.

In the process of cleansing the water, however, all the junk that was in the water gets centrifuged into a greasy, contaminated mass: sludge. The better the wastewater treatment, the worse the sludge. This can, and does, include synthetic chemicals that don't break down; all the bugs that cause diseases like salmonella, cholera, and schistomaisis, to name a few; heavy metals; and the residues of all the drugs we humans take to try and be healthy.

Americans produce about 7,000,000 dry tons of sludge a year, and there it sits, filled with disease vectors and chemicals invented by scientists who failed to factor in the effects of their synthetic compounds on the water supply and soil, not to mention the ocean itself.

In principle, this sludge—more delicately called biosolids in America—can be recycled into good, clean fertilizer by heating it up to 70°C, killing all the pathogens in it, and making it safe for use as fertilizer in parks, schoolyards, and agricultural land. In practice, however, it is not so clear that this new fertilizer is completely clear of pathogens, as people living close to fields where it is spread have been getting sick at unprecedented rates. It is a work-in-progress. I hope that since our species is technologically savvy enough to go to the moon, that we will work out how to recycle our waste products effectively, preferably in low-tech ways. In this spirit, it is my most fervent prayer that the Sludge People talk to Fungi People, especially to Paul Stamets, who I consider to be one of our national treasures.

Mushrooms

Mycologist Paul Stamets[4] is the author of *Mycelium Running: How Mushrooms Can Save the World* and uses mushrooms to bioremediate toxic waste, which he calls "mycoremediation." He says that even though people are very good at inventing toxins, we're not so good at eliminating them. (Sadly, I wish we had thought of this when we split the atom, or when we began breaking apart the DNA molecule. Or drilled for oil in the Gulf of Mexico.)

It turns out that fungi have the ability to break down toxic molecules by secreting digestive enzymes that digest liquin and cellulose, disrupting the chemical bonds in a wide range of toxins. They convert cellulose to fungal sugars, thereby rendering the toxins harmless. This may sound too good to be true, but by running a test at the Department of Defense facility on four same-sized piles of diesel-contaminated soil, one next to the other Stamets showed that it *was* true.

One pile was inoculated with layers of oyster mushroom spawn in sawdust, two of the other piles were given bacterial treatments, and the fourth pile was the control pile. All the piles were then covered with shade cloth and black plastic tarps against rain, and left for four weeks. At the end of that time, three piles were found to be as black and lifeless as before, stinking of oil, but the pile that had been treated with oyster mushroom spawn was covered with mushrooms, and the now-fragrant soil had turned a light brown!

What was most amazing to Stamets was what came next: an ecosystem began to form around the mushroom-treated soil! As the fungi began to putrefy, they attracted insects that laid their eggs in the now-viable soil. Their larvae attracted birds, and the winds brought airborne seeds that took root in the soil and sprouted. Within six weeks, that pile of previously oil-saturated soil was teeming with healthy green life. It flowered and attracted butterflies, then bees. And to their amazement, says Stamets, after doing the tests, they found that the oyster mushrooms contained no toxicity at all and were actually edible. He refers to this experiment as a "life gateway" and has continued to search for mushrooms that can be used in bioremediation.

Flu viruses, coliform bacteria, and smallpox pathogens can also be rendered harmless in various ways by mycelia. Fertilizers, munitions, pesticides, herbicides, dyes, and estrogen-based pharmaceuticals are all susceptible to the enzymes the fungi secrete. Heavy metals can be absorbed, petroleum hydrocarbons, industrial wastes, wood that has been treated with arsenic...The list goes on and on.

My friend Enrique, grower of those opuntia cactus *nopales*, picked up some of this treated wood at the dump to try out Stamets' claim, built a chair out of it, inoculated it with shiitake mushroom spores, and put it out on the porch to see what would happen. His wife Miki rolled her eyes, but eventually the chair indeed bore fruit, producing a rich harvest of edible mushrooms that we all ate one night for dinner—and lived to tell the tale.

Stamets has also designed burlap-bag dams to place downstream from farms using pesticides and herbicides. He uses storm debris to fill each sack, then inoculates the filled sacs with mushroom spores that fruit and actually catch the toxins leached into the stream water. This man's ingenuity seems to know no bounds.

We had a toxic oil spill on our beloved San Francisco Bay a few years ago, and because of the toxicity of the muck, citizens were not allowed to do independent cleanup for the critical first days of the spill. And then I learned that Paul Stamets had raced to the rescue with "hair mats!" Putting out a call to barbers, hairdressers, and animal breeders across the country, he accumulated massive piles of hair that were made into floating mats and dropped by boats onto the worst of the spill, sopping up the sticky black goo and debris. When the mats were saturated, they were collected by boat and piled up on the shore where they were innoculated with mushroom spore. In a few weeks, the hairy piles were covered in mushrooms. Eventually, the whole mess was transformed into soil, with its succession of insects, plants, and birds.

Much closer to home, one thing we can all do is to comb our hair outdoors, weather permitting, and allow our stray hairs to land where they will as an offering to the local birds. During nesting season, your hairs will become the softest linings for bird nests!

Paul Stamets says, "We can engage mycelium to help save the world!" To that, I say a resounding Yes! especially when Stamets dreams up ideas like the Life Box. He suggests that all cardboard—delivery cartons, toilet roll cylinders, and so on—be impregnated with mycelia spores when they are manufactured. Then, instead of either dumping or recycling the cardboard that comes through our doors everyday, we put it in the garden, add some soil, water it, and wait for the mushrooms to come. Add lettuce seeds, and we have planted a garden; add pinecones, why then we may have planted a forest.

He claims that researchers at Yeshiva University are discovering that fungi with melanin—skin pigment that darkens when exposed to sunlight—use radiation the way green plants use chlorophyll. The implications of this, of course, are staggering. Stay tuned.

This man thinks big, and he also thinks small. Mushrooms, he points out, can be grown in discarded coffee grounds—espresso makes the best—and discarded corn cobs make a perfect fruiting medium; even carpenter ant bodies, believe it or not, will sprout mushrooms under certain conditions. Take a look at *Mycellium Running* to find out more about the carpenter ants.

You can grow your own mushrooms by inoculating sawdust, woodchips, or logs, indoors or out, depending upon the amount of space you have. It's a wonderful project to do with children. Paul's business, Fungi Perfecti, shows you how, and will sell you the spawn. For more information, check the resources section at the end of this chapter.

Landfills and Dumps

When our children were small, an excursion to the Berkeley City Dump down by the San Francisco Bay in California was a favorite outing for bird watching and sunsets. And the views!

The birds and views are still there, but what once was a smelly municipal dump is now a 90-acre park, with a waterfront, hillsides, groves of trees, wheelchair-accessible pathways, and hidden trails. Dogs chase after frisbees, and kites sail in the wind. Children learn to ride bikes, and joggers jog. Wildlife has been moving in—herons and hawks, snakes and burrowing owls; occasionally, you can spot a harbor seal out in the water. And on the trails you hear people speaking every language in the world.

I remember being part of a ritual circle with a group of friends atop one of the garbage heaps about 20 years ago, just after the Waterfront Commission had voted to turn the Berkeley City Dump into Cesar Chavez Park.[5] Beneath my feet were twisted nylon stockings and cigarette butts, rusted tin cans and Pepsi bottles—this was before recycling. It was hard to imagine all this trash turning into parkland, but we held hands and sang together and dreamed of green. Now it's hard to imagine that the park hasn't been there since the beginning of time.

Adventurers' Playground

Not far from Cesar Chavez Park is a little bit of kid heaven that looks, at first glance, like a junkyard. It is, but it is a deliberate junkyard where children can hammer and saw and paint and climb and crawl around structures made out of scrap wood, discarded tires, old cargo nets—all built by the kids themselves. Although each child must come with an adult, he or she is not supervised by the adult but trusted to be able to wield a hammer safely and climb to the top of a rope ladder alone.

This playground makes me want to be a kid again so I could bang away to my heart's content, plunk at the broken innards of the old baby grand in the "noise sculpture," ride the various rope swings, and disappear inside one of the crazy-quilt castles of wood kids have collectively built over the years. The way I can participate, though, is to recycle all my wood scraps there, after I've removed the nails, of course. Another case of stacked functions.

Compost

Your compost heap at home may be on a different scale from the landfill, but the idea is the same. Starting with trash—in this case, organic plant matter—you encourage it to break down and transform itself back into soil by accumulating it, keeping it wet and warm, and aerating it by turning it from time to time. Its smell is earthy and rich—quite pleasant, in fact—a sign that waste has become usable soil rather than garbage. At our house, we've had to request a smaller-size trash receptacle from the city because we produce so little trash. After recycling all our paper, glass, tin, and plastic and putting our kitchen scraps into the compost, there's precious little left to pick up.

For years, our compost heap was piled in the backyard and received everything from kitchen scraps to weeds and clippings from the garden. We gave it a turn every now and then, exposing fragrant new soil and a million happy worms, and every spring would transfer the whole thing to the vegetable beds in front.

Then we learned of vermiculture, composting with the aid of worms, which has turned us into great worm enthusiasts. We set up a worm bin in a corner of the garden, were given a handful of red worms from a friend's stash. Now, several gazillion squirmy little guys are multiplying at a great rate in our worm bin, slurping their way through the fungi and bacteria breaking down our pineapple skin and cabbage leaves, turning our slops into the best fertilizer in the world.

The wonderful thing about vermiculture is that you don't need a garden to compost your kitchen wastes—a self-contained box in the basement or a deep closet will do it. I know one woman who keeps it under the kitchen table. All the worms request is moisture and replenishment, then they are happy to be left alone to multiply and do their thing.

Mary Appelhof,[6] recently deceased, wrote the definitive book on vermicomposting. *Worms Eat my Garbage: How to Set Up and Maintain a Vermicomposting System* is the first and last word on redworms. It is written for children as well as adults, tells you everything you need to know about worms—including their sex lives—and goes at it with such relish that you'll want to run right out and get your own worm bin. I met her once and was so impressed by this passionate woman that I did just that. I have never looked back.

Junk Into Art

Methane stacks protrude here and there from trees and tall grasses at the waterfront park that used to be our city dump, releasing the gas that accumulates from all that decomposition. My only regret is that we are not using it. I think of Calabash! and the artists turning gourds into artworks, and I wonder how artists might have used this gas to create kinetic sculptures with moving parts.

If my friend Adrienne—she of the bread sculptures—still lived in the Bay Area, she no doubt would have been one of them, as this is the kind of challenge that sparks her creative soul. She loves haunting places like Urban Ore,[7] which sells secondhand stuff such as building supplies, furniture, and appliances, and the Creative Re-Use Depot,[8] which sells, as creative art materials, everything else.

One year, Adrienne and I went thrift-store shopping together to create an outdoor sculpture that made music, keeping an eye out for potential percussion instruments. This did not mean actual musical instruments, she assured me, but things that satisfyingly went *clunk* and *bang*. Our plan was to build a sound sculpture to hang from a particular oak tree on land in the country owned by people we knew. They had given us permission to create our sculpture near the garden, although they confessed they had no idea exactly what we had in mind. Actually, neither did I, but Adrienne assured me that she did, so off we went on a search for things that made noise.

We had the most engrossing time scavenging in and out of dusty yards and dimly lit shops, and at the end of the day our arms were loaded with treasures. We found a single Ziljan cymbal, slightly cracked but perfect for our purposes; old silver knives, forks, and spoons; the rim of a bicycle wheel; a variety of pot lids; actual castanets; several lengths of bamboo and a variety of rusted wind-chimes and tinkling doo-dads. We spent well under 15 dollars for the lot. Then we went up to the country and set to work.

Every part of the process was great fun, from crashing and banging everything together to test it for sound, to hanging each piece strategically in a grand old oak tree. We had such a good time that we wondered if a creative imagination and a good friend might be all that any of us needs to be happy in this world.

We strung the bamboo so that it struck the cymbal just so when the wind blew from the east, and the bicycle wheel brushed across the forks and spoons when it was spun. Pipes *dinged* against each other in the breeze, and the castanets *clunked* satisfyingly when they hit the pot lids. For several days, Adrienne and I laughed our heads off while we worked, and when it was finished, recorded our sound sculpture. I still listen to it when I am having trouble sleeping. The folks there were amazed, and as far as I know, are still showing off our crazy sound sculpture created by "two women who made something out of nothing."

Art at the Dump

In 1990, the San Francisco Solid Waste Transfer and Recycling Center (aka the Dump)[9] began hosting artists-in-residence for four-month residencies, during which time each artist scavenges through piles of trash and create works of art from what he or she finds there. Artists are given studio space and an exhibition of their work, which then becomes part of a permanent collection available for exhibit locally and nationally.

Composer Nathaniel Stookey was one artist-in-residence there. He collected pots and pans, beer bottles, oil drums and garbage cans, water jugs and old saws, buckets and pipes, shopping carts and car fenders, and created music for an eight-member percussion ensemble called Junkestra.[10] I heard them perform at Symphony Hall recently and especially loved the sound that the soles of flip-flops have on five-gallon water jugs—not to mention how silver forks, in the hands of masters, can really "git down" on the sides of a shopping cart!

The current artist-in-residence, Ben Burke, has created rafts out of discarded materials and sailed them down the Mississippi River, the Hudson River, and the Adriatic Sea, bringing awareness to the issue of trash recyclability. "Upcycling," it is called. In the current show, puppet installations made of everything from mannequins to old pianos move their heads and reach out with arms, lighting up at the press of a button and whirring into life, evoking childhood dreams and nightmares.

In a Museum of Crafts in Charlotte, North Carolina, I came upon the remarkable work of Boris Bally,[11] who creates jewelry from plastic debris. His statement above the exhibit read, "... the greatest challenge is to make something from trash or discards seem 'sexy' or 'valuable.'"

I found his work witty and beautiful and looked forward to trying some of his techniques myself. Then, a few days later, I came across a heartbreaking photograph in a magazine, of a dead albatross chick decomposing on a beach. What was *not* decomposing, however, were the contents of its stomach—brightly colored plastic debris, exactly like the debris in Bally's necklaces. Mistaking these shiny baubles for nutritious food, the chick's parent had apparently brought them back to the nest, systematically starving its young. I sat down and wept.

If only ... if only we *all* collected plastic junk and made necklaces like Bally's, then we might have kept some of it out of the ocean and out of the gullets of young seabirds. If only we were not so unconscious, maybe we wouldn't blithely toss junk over our shoulders without a backward glance. If only we had collectively been more conscious, maybe we wouldn't have invented nonbiodegradable stuff in the first place.

Recently, when I mentioned to a friend who has taught chemistry for decades how I felt about chemists inventing polymers without taking into account what happened to plastic later, he was stunned. "I never thought of that," he muttered finally. His eyes were sad.

In Crete, my friend Aliki Zaimaki tells me that people have always thrown their orange peels and cigarette butts onto the ground, where they disappeared underfoot sooner or later. Now, though, even though there are many more people and most things are made from nonbiodegradable plastic or metal, people continue to throw trash on the ground. She says, sadly, that the place is filthy, and people don't seem to notice the difference.

I take the problem of trash seriously enough to go down to San Francisco Bay periodically with bucket and work gloves to pick up junk at Emery Cove. I find plastic bottle caps, waterbottles, cigarette filters. I find smaller and smaller bits of styrofoam mixing with the sand. I find beer bottles and food wrappers, broken plastic toys and rubber gloves.

Michelle Obama has suggested we all volunteer to do something for our community, and this is the task I have designated for myself. Often, I make a play-date out of it, inviting a friend to do it with me, and as we pick over the beach we hang out and talk. Then when the beach is presentable again, we take our picnic basket to the jetty, and over lunch stare out at the waves. It takes about two hours every few weeks to clear the cove. No, I don't have the heart to turn it into art—I just toss it in the trash barrels and pray it doesn't end up back in the bay.

One of my closest friends is the artist Sharon Strong,[12] who *does* make use of junk in her art, both as an artist and as a psychologist. Her canvas is the human face, and she creates masks that reveal, rather than conceal, what is hidden on the inside. The process is revelatory, and the results are invariably stunning.

Sharon once set herself the challenge of creating 20 masks using her own face, in order to explore her relation to the natural world. She wanted to express in these masks who she was as a woman, a member of the human community and as a part of Nature. It was an extraordinary tour de force. Her inspirations, she said, came from things she found at her feet.

Taking a walk with her and seeing the world through her eyes is always a treat. She doesn't miss a thing. An unusual piece of burned wood becomes the antlers of an archetypal elk; twisted wire, a dried palm frond, feathers, tortoise shells, and wood ear fungi all become transformed into recognizable people—you and me—at every stage of our lives. As Sharon puts it: "I was seeing masks everywhere in Nature—in feathers and bones, tree fungus, rusty bottle caps, and a beetle carcass. In a frenzy of creativity, everything I touched came alive in one mask after another."

Sharon takes mask-making into the world, working with schools and juvenile halls, recovering alcoholics and abused women—the so-called "waste" of our society. She has people work in pairs to life-cast each other's faces, to create the face-form upon which they will each make a mask. They all then create symbolic portraits of themselves—their fears and dreams—upon their personal mask, using whatever significant bits and pieces of their history help tell their story. The results, as you might imagine, are extraordinary.

Artist Jerry Wennstrom,[13] from Whidbey Island in Washington State, may be the world's foremost upcyler. His larger-than-life sculptures are made entirely of scavenged materials found at the dump, or come from friends who are on the lookout for him. When I purged my house of outdated "stuff," he received more than one package from me.

Jerry started out as a successful painter in New York City, where his paintings were exhibited at museums and sold for thousands of dollars. But he says that something essential was missing for him, so he gave away or burned all his art, left his apartment, and took to the road in a soul-search for that ineffable *something*. For 15 years he wandered, following the four winds and dependent upon the generosity of others, until he cast up on the shores of Whidbey Island, where he decided it was time to settle.

He lives there now with his wonderful wife Marilyn, tucked quietly in the woods where he transforms abandoned junk into profound and whimsical art. He makes many-layered sculptures that look like sarcophagi with moving parts that chatter and clack, burst open and twirl. He laughs along with you as you press one of the many buttons and a whole Rube Goldberg scene starts whirring and ringing, doors popping open, and breasts handing out fortunes. His pieces are wild and wacky inventions, ingenious fun from head to toe.

In the woods outside his basement gallery of characters is the couple's tiny meditation treehouse. It's made from salvaged wood and reached via a pebble-pathway composed of shattered, round-edged bits of windshield glass that tinkle beneath your feet as you walk. Jerry is a happy man whose sense of humor never quits. Every piece he does is devotional, and every piece he does breathes with imagination and life. And everything is created from waste.

Patchwork Quilts

A while ago, when I was going through a hard time because so many people I knew were dying, my friend Snoo Heslen—who was terminally ill and one of the reasons I was having a hard time—advised me to take up quilting. She told me, from her sickbed, that working with colored fabric would help calm me under stress and keep my hands and mind busy. She gave me several bags of scraps from her own projects and taught me how to use them. Then she bequeathed to me my favorite of her quilts—a blue, orange, and red double nine-patch that will always be my favorite comfort quilt—and watched as I composed and pieced my first quilt-top.

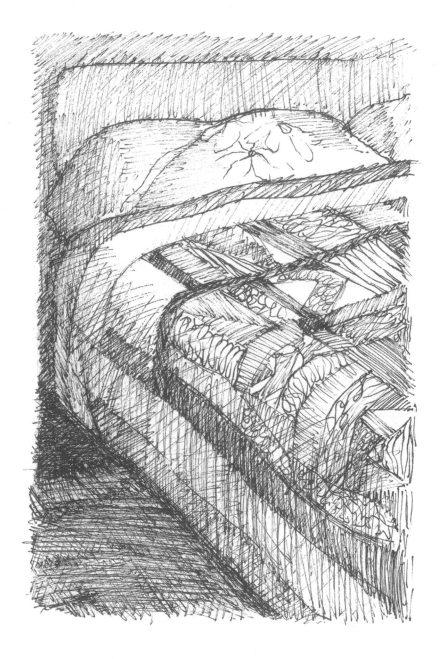

Snoo is gone, but I have followed her advice and now use quilting as my stress-management of choice. She was from the school of traditional designs pieced precisely, but I am from more of the "crazy-quilt" school of quilting. In fact, I prefer to use only the fabrics that come my way, willy-nilly—a bit the way Jerry works. Fabric comes to me from people's scrap bags and worn-out clothes, faded tablecloths, and old curtains. For me, the game is to make do with what I have, revising the design accordingly.

People often enjoy playing the game with me, and from time to time I find a sack of scraps on my porch from someone who has recently cleaned house. I love having no choice but to be inventive with color and quantity, substituting fuchsia when I run out of orange, or making a thin purple border when I only have a small amount of purple. If I've got a bigger piece of brown, then the wide border next to it may well be brown. Then I step back to see the effect of fuchsia and orange, purple and brown. More often than not, I'm thrilled.

I've been told that my quilts are unique, but I've discovered to my deep delight that I actually belong to a long tradition. Until I saw a collection of African American quilts a few years ago, I had no idea they existed. Wildly colorful and imaginative, these quilters play with shape and materials in ways that I do: they start with a color scheme and/or a design idea and then improvise on the theme. Pretty much anything goes, and surprises and accidents are part of the process. The results are invariably gorgeous—and so alive.

The ones I know best are the quilts made by the women of Gee's Bend, Alabama.[14] In an isolated bend of the river, not far from Selma, six generations of women have been making quilts to keep their families warm through the winters, passing their craft down from mother to daughter.

Made from worn dungarees and the non-threadbare parts of old aprons, from gunny-sacks and outgrown dresses, from old shirts and shiny ties, each quilt is a unique work of art. The quilter starts with an idea, a palate of color, and then takes off. A regular pattern will suddenly veer off into a whimsical counterpoint of itself; lines and circles, squares and stripes appear right-side up and then upside down; a blue border suddenly changes into a red one. Asymmetry is the name of the game. And each is its own composition, recognizable and satisfying. Their quilts made me laugh and then cry.

Each of these women works by herself piecing her quilt top, following her own artistic vision, and then a community of women come together to put top, batting and backing together—"making the sandwich." They sew and talk, sing and laugh, helping each other through all the weathers and all the hard times, making sure that each of them has warm blankets for her children. A girl getting married is sent to her new life with a quilt made by the women of her clan. It is a work of the heart that they are engaged in, and the beauty they create is breathtaking.

Building with Straw

At Daily Bread, ideas and offers often come our way unsolicited, and when they do we make a point of taking advantage of them. When a cocoa manufacturer went out of business, we delivered bags of cocoa to every food kitchen in town; when we were offered a small plot of land in the city, we made a garden. And when rice growers had to stockpile, rather than burn their rice straw chaff, we dreamed up a house.

On the same land Adrienne and I had created our sound sculpture, my husband Herb and I received permission, in 1990, to build a small strawbale cottage for ourselves and other visitors to the land, if we funded the project. This was not an opportunity to be turned down, especially as a load-bearing building of straw had not been officially permitted by building departments in the United States at that time. If this worked, it might possibly offset the rapacious clear-cutting of our forests, and I felt the risk was worth taking.

Rice straw is high in silica content and does not break down easily. Rice growers had long burned it, creating severe air pollution that had resulted in a burn ban in the Bay Area. The stockpiled chaff was now taking up too much productive land, and rice growers were searching for alternatives.

Sponsored officially by Daily Bread, along with visionary architect Bob Theis, we took on the task of designing and building with an agricultural waste product—a rice strawbale house that would demonstrate straw as a viable building material.[15] We hoped to update building codes to reflect that, help save some number of trees, and create a beautiful and cozy weekend place in the country for ourselves and others.

It was a hard job but extraordinary fun. The hardest part was not the building of the house but convincing skeptics that the house would not fall down—we heard a lot about the three little pigs that year. The permitting process, which took over a year, was the hardest part of all. Everything had to be tested and retested, and we had to provide extensive engineering evidence that the house would not collapse or burn easily. This brought out amazing ingenuity on everyone's parts, and the adventure of designing with thick straw walls, shaping them, and playing around with mud on a construction site with strong, visionary builders, both men and women, was thrilling to me.

The rice straw was reused material, but so was everything else in the house. Our goal was to demonstrate a gracious, small home in which everything: windows, doors, stairs, floor, kitchen were made of secondhand materials. The floor would be the mud taken from the site mixed with linseed oil, and most of the furniture would be built into deep-set window-seats.

Our working plan was to create a blueprint of the basic structure and then to improvise the details as we went along, turning every nook and cranny into something useful. Needless to say we made many mistakes—nobody had ever done this before— but every mistake suggested an ingenious solution. My favorite part, in fact, was the hours spent brainstorming in the evenings around a fire, with all the volunteer builders who showed up from everywhere to help and learn about building with straw.

The result was a beautiful, state-of-the-art little house that made building history, provided a smart alternative to the rice-growers' dilemma, and helped change the building codes around the country. Straw bale construction is now an accepted option to building with wood, and is being used as far away as Mongolia and as close as our gorgeous little getaway in wine-growing country. It could be a place to grow old in.

Over My Dead Body!

When plants die, they drop their leaves and stems and seedpods to the earth, providing for the next year's growth; when animals die, they are eaten by fellow creatures who grow fat on their flesh; when humans die, well, that's another can of worms—literally, as well as figuratively.

On land that used to be outside the city limits of New York City, grave plots in a series of cemeteries now go on for miles inside those city limits. I imagine it was once good farming land. Beneath the ground are the mottled bones of our ancestors, encased in decaying caskets leaching formaldehyde-laced embalming fluids into the earth with the rains of decades. As time goes on, and more of us are born and die, I wonder where they will put us all?

This is the ultimate waste problem: what to do with *ourselves* when we die? Historically, bodies have been buried in the ground, buried in the sea, left out on mountaintops, placed on high towers for vultures, or cremated. Different cultures have different practices of transferring the elements of our physical bodies from one form to another while our souls awaken to their next stage of development, and each practice has its problems as our numbers accumulate.

Modern burial in watertight caskets not only takes up more and more land but also slows the natural decomposition of the body, preventing the fertilization of the earth around it. Biodegradable caskets are now available, and some cemeteries allow burial straight into the ground, but the space to put the body is still an issue. Cremations are a good idea, but immense amounts of energy are used for the burning. Not many of us, not to mention the earth, can afford this.

A new procedure, called Alkaline Hydrolysis, places the corpse into a stainless steel chamber with potassium hydroxide and water heated to 300 degrees, and essentially scrubs the body until the flesh and soft tissue have dissolved. The bones are then pulverized into ash, and returned to the family, while the liquid goes safely, so they say, down the drain. I wonder, though, about the amounts of fresh water used and the fuels that heat the water to 300 degrees. We cannot really afford that, either.

When I was last in India's holy city of Benares, we saw corpses on burning pyres melting in the heat of the flames—that is, when the families of the deceased had the means to purchase a full load of wood; we also saw half-burned corpses floating in the River Ganges, when the families did not.

Towers of Silence, such as those the Zoroastrians in India use for their dead; sky burials on mountaintops, still traditionally used in Tibet; and burials at sea make sense in context, but I can't quite imagine any of these methods playing in Kansas—or London, for that matter. I have no easy solutions, but I bring up the issue because it is an issue.

For myself, I can only hope that when my time comes I have the nerve and mobility to somehow get to the sea, and with the love of friends and family, walk in until the waves take me. I would like very much, as my last act on Earth, to provide a meal for a white shark, perhaps giving her the extra *oompf* she needs to evade a fishing net, where she would be separated from her fin for the sharks-fin soup trade, the rest of her body left to die slowly and painfully. Oh yes, that would give me great satisfaction.

Sigh. We have got to learn how to close the loops; to come full circle; to reuse creatively; to imagine new possibilities. We've got to think as big as Nature does, using everything and wasting nothing.

The ethnographer Wade Davis, in *Light at the Edge of the World*, describes the race between stingless bees, metallic flies, and scarab beetles, in the forests of Borneo, for every bit of dung deposited on the forest floor. They return it to the food chain within hours. It is, he says, "scat reduced to shadow."

I wonder: how long might it take them to reduce a human corpse to shadow?

> *Fallen petals of red plum*
> *Are like fires burning*
> *On the clods of horse-shit.*
> —BUSON

ADDITIONAL INSPIRATIONS

Green America is a not-for-profit membership organization founded in 1982. It was known as Co-op America until January 1, 2009. The organization's mission is to harness economic power—the strength of consumers, investors, businesses, and the marketplace—to create a socially just and environmentally sustainable society. Green America works for a world where all people have enough, where all communities are healthy and safe, and where the bounty of the earth is preserved for all the generations to come. For more information, visit *www.greenamericatoday.org*

It also sends out a fact sheet entitled: *Things You Didn't Know You Could Recycle*. Most of us know about paper and glass and tin can recyclables, some plastics, and in some cities, green recycling that goes into county composting efforts. But we can recycle a lot more, including, for example:

- appliances: *www.goodwill.org*
- steel: *www.recycle-steel.org*
- athletic shoes: *www.oneworldrunning.com; www.nikereuseashoe.com*
- batteries: *www.batteryrecycling.com*
- compact fluorescent bulbs*: www.ikea.com, www.sylvania.com/recycle/recyclepak*
- computers and electronics: *www.ban.org/pledge/Locations.html*
- Foam packing peanuts: *www.epspackaging.org/info.html*
- ink/toner cartridges: *www.recycleplace.com*
- motor oil: *www.recycleoil.org_*
- telephones: *www.donateaphone.com*
- For more information, visit *www.greenamerica.org*

The Freecycle Network™ is made up of 4,793 groups with 7,208,000 members across the globe. It's a grassroots and entirely nonprofit movement of people who are giving (and getting) stuff for free in their own towns. It's all about reuse and keeping good stuff out of landfills. Membership is free. To locate your local branch of Freecycle.org, visit *www.freecycle.org*

Zoo Poopy Doo is an exotic way to fertilize your garden through a unique method of recycling waste from zoo animals. At the Louisville Zoo in Kentucky, Zoo Poopy Doo™ was introduced by assistant zoo director Mark Zoeller. It consists of manure from animals such as elephants, rhinos, camels, and giraffes, which is blended with hay, straw, and wood shavings. Experts at the zoo say it improves the aeration of soil and increases root penetration and water retention, which together reduces crusting of the soil surface.

At Woodland Park Zoo in Seattle, Washington, where Zoo Doo™ has been offered since the early 1990s, they speak of their "endangered feces." Manure and straw bedding are collected from animal enclosures and combined with other natural recyclable materials from around the zoo to compost. The heating up in the composting process kills most weed seeds and pathogens. The product is turned and watered for three months until it becomes dry and crumbly. It is ready then to be sold as fertilizer. For more information, visit *www.zoo.org/zoo-doo* or *www.zoodoo.co.nz/*

Adrienne Robinson is an artist who creates in a wide variety of media. She especially loves working with found objects. Adrienne and I have collaborated many times over the years, most recently on an exhibition and book of creation myths titled *In the Beginning: Creation Myths From Around The World* (ICRL Press 2010). For more information, visit *www.icrl.org*

ENDNOTES

1. **Toby Hemenway** is the author of the first major North American book on permaculture, Gaia's Garden: A Guide to Home-Scale Permaculture. His website includes information on permaculture workshops and courses, principles of permaculture, an extensive reading list, articles, and links. For more information, visit *www.patternliteracy.com*

2. **Rose George** is currently associate editor for *Tank,* a quarterly magazine of fashion, art, reportage, and culture based in London, and the author of *"The Big Necessity: The Unmentionable World of Human Waste and Why It Matters"* (Holt Paperback 2008). For more information, visit *http://rosegeorge.com/site/books/the-big-necessity*

3. **Wade Davis** is an ethnographer, writer, photographer, filmmaker, and ethnobotanist, He spent more than three years in the Amazon and Andes as a plant explorer, living among 15 indigenous groups in eight Latin American nations while making some 6,000 botanical collections. His work later took him to Haiti to investigate folk preparations implicated in the creation of zombies, For more information, visit *http://www.nationalgeographic.com/field/explorers/wade-davis.html*

4. **Paul Stamets** is the author of numerous books and papers on the subject of mushroom identification and cultivation, Stamets has discovered four new species of mushrooms. He is an advocate of the permaculture system of growing, and considers fungiculture a valuable but underutilized aspect of permaculture. He is also a leading researcher into the use of mushrooms in bioremediation, processes he terms mycoremediation and mycofiltration. His work was featured in the documentary film *The 11th Hour.* For more information, visit *www.fungi.com*

5. **Cesar Chavez Park** is located at 11 Spinnaker Way, north of the west end of University Avenue, Marina/Northwest Berkeley. Built on the site of a former landfill, it offers a wide range of recreational opportunities in a marina setting, with spectacular views of the three bay bridges, Alcatraz, and Angel Island. For more information, visit *http://www.ci.berkeley.ca.us/ContentDisplay.aspx?id=12102*

6. **Mary Appelhopf** spent her life developing products and services that use earthworms to convert organic waste, such as banana peels, bread crusts, and coffee grounds, to rich compost. The process is called "vermicomposting."

Appelhof wrote articles on vermicomposting, published a popular book on worm composting, and designed the Worm-a-Way™ composter for home use. Appelhof died on May 4, 2005. For more information, visit *www.wormwoman.com*

7.   **Urban Ore** was formed to end the age of waste by advocating and developing total recycling. They receive unwanted things and sells them as-is for reuse. They design disposal facilities for zero waste and publish technical papers. For more information, visit *http://urbanore.ypguides.net*

8.   **The Creative Reuse Depot** is an ecological treasure trove of art and craft materials, educational supplies, vintage furniture, home décor, paper goods, fabric, and much more. Their mission is to divert waste materials from landfills by collecting and redistributing discarded goods as low-cost supplies for art, education, and social services. For more information, visit *www.creativereuse.org*

9,10.   **Recology**, combining the practices of recycling and ecology, is a program at city dumps that reclaims useful materials from the trash and make them available to citizens. In San Francisco, it runs a program for artists-in-residence who make use of trash for their artforms. The junk orchestra, Junkestra, was created by Nathaniel Stookey who collected his sonorous stash by heading onto city trash piles in a helmet, safety goggles, gloves, and steel-shank boots and, amid giant moving tractors, tested the musical potential of discarded objects. He then placed his findings in a shopping cart, which he pushed down city streets back to his studio. "I had no idea when I started writing this piece how beautiful the instruments could sound. It just sounds like a very strange, exotic orchestra." For more information about recology and the artist-in-residence program, visit *http://sunsetscavenger.com/AIR/stookey.htm*

11.   **Boris Bally's** work employs the use of jeweler's skills on nonprecious materials and is both witty and innovative. His current body of work transforms recycled street signs, weapon parts, and a wide variety of found materials into objects for reflection. These pieces celebrate raw American street-aesthetic in the form of objects, often useful, for the home and the body. For more information, visit *www.borisbally.com*

12.   **Sharon Strong** is a practicing clinical psychologist in the foothills of Northern California, and a painter, performance artist, and maker of masks. She says: "As a psychologist, I've spent years reading people's expressions, noticing the subtleties that play across their faces. I reflect back what I see. This helps people experience a deeper reality of themselves. We usually think of masks as conceal-ing, 'wearing a mask.' As an artist, I want to reveal what is underneath our masks. I love the paradox!" For more information, visit *www.beneaththemask. com*

13. **Jerry Wennstrom** is an artist and author from New York City who began as a studio painter and at the height of his career destroyed all of his art and gave away everything he owned. He began a life of unconditional trust, allowing life to provide all that was needed and lived that way for 15 years. He now lives and works on Whidbey Island in Washington State. For more information, visit *www.handsofalchemy.com*

14. **Gee's Bend Quilts.** The women of the Gee's Bend Quilters Collective all live in the area of Rehoboth and Boykin, Alabama. The women consider the process of "piecing" the quilt "top" to be highly personal. In Gee's Bend, the top—the side that faces up on the bed—is always pieced by a quilter working alone and reflects a singular artistic vision. The subsequent process of "quilting" the quilt—sewing together the completed top, the batting (stuffing), and the back—is sometimes then performed communally, among small groups of women. Most of the quilters were featured in the book *Gee's Bend: The Women And Their Quilts* (Tinwood 2002), where extensive biographical information can be found. For more information, visit *www.quiltsofgeesbend.com*

15. **Straw Bale Building.** *The Last Straw* (TLS), is the international journal of straw-bale and natural building since 1993. You can order back issues and current issues from their website and also view a calendar of events, including workshops and training opportunities; classified listings for jobs and apprenticeships, real estate, and items you want to find or sell. For more information, visit www.strawhomes.com or *www.greenbuilder.com*. To see the house built by my family, check out my website *http://www.healingimprovisations.net*. Look under "Social Activism."

CHAPTER FOUR

WATER

*Waters are spring and origin, the reservoir of all
the possibilities of existence; they precede every
form and support every creation.*
—*MIRCEA ELIADE*

When I was about 17 years old and still living at home in New York City, I got my boyfriend John to take me out to the beach during a winter storm. I think we were at that bravado stage of our relationship in which he wanted to impress me, and I was testing his devotion, so he consented, even though the night was cold and the subway ride to Coney Island long.

Nobody else was on the beach, of course, and the sea was a wild thing, crashing and pounding on the shore, the wind shrieking and the foam flying. I was thrilled!

"Don't you just *love* the mystery of the sea?" I shouted, as he huddled deep in his overcoat, wool hat pulled low over his ears and his face a picture of patient misery. Poor guy. Well, he got back at me for dragging him out there, by shouting back, "No, I don't! That's being ignorant! What you should love is wave mechanics and the movement of water molecules and how the wind affects the waves!" He was yelling over the din of the sea. "It's *not* a mystery!"

That stopped me cold. Maybe he was right; after all, he was the Harvard physics major, not me. Freezing cold out there, we soon left the beach and went home, both of us a bit chastened now. We spoke little on the way back, and our relationship eventually ended, but what I would like to say to him now is that I see that water is both: it is wave mechanics and molecules, *and* it is mystery. We were both right.

Sacred Water

Ancient Chinese sages proclaim that "water is love." In Arabic, *Aman d'Imam* means "water is life." In the Bible, in the Book of Genesis, God creates a firmament in the midst of the waters, and in the Book of Job, it says, "though a tree be cut down ... yet through the scent of water it will bud."

According to the belief systems of many ancient and indigenous cultures, water was conscious and sacred, the source of life and health for all living beings. Without water, there would be no life. Water was how the physical world merged with the spirit world, and in creation myths symbolized the primordial matrix from which the whole world was created.

The understanding of water as sacred has unfortunately gotten lost in its commodification. We seem to have forgotten that we are part of a living web of Nature, dependent upon its plants and animals and minerals for our sustenance and the very air we breathe. We are born of water, and we need to be sustained by water. Our bodies are over 70 percent water; they will not survive for more than a few days without the input of fresh water. As Aristotle has said, "Water is the first principle of life." More recently, Theodor Schwenk,[1] author of *Sensitive Chaos*, a treatise about water, tells us that the ancients understood "living water" to be the only way of mediating between the invisible realms and the physical world.

Facts and Figures

Here are some facts about water that will put into perspective everything that follows:

- The 326 million cubic miles of water on the planet that were created 3 billion years ago, following the Big Bang, are still in existence and continue to cycle as gas, liquid, and ice through time.
- Water covers more than 71 percent of the earth's surface.
- 97 percent of the world's water is in the sea, and 2 percent is locked up in the polar ice caps, glaciers, and deep aquifers.
- The remaining 1 percent of freshwater on the planet is all that is available to sustain all living beings, including ourselves.
- 20 percent of this 1 percent remaining freshwater is in Lake Baikal in Siberia.
- A full one-half of the 1 percent of freshwater on the planet has been polluted by humans and rendered unusable for life. The main source of pollution is excrement; others are chemical, thermal, physical, and radioactive materials.

- The amount of water used to produce food and goods imported by developed countries is worsening water shortages in the developing world.
- The ratio of water in the human body is the same as that on the planet.
- The average person contains about 100 pounds of water in the body, and we use our body weight of water every four weeks.
- Every person living in a city makes direct use of between 100 and 150 gallons of freshwater a day, much of which returns, contaminated, to the city's sewers, and eventually to the sea.
- Without water we would die from dehydration in a few days. A loss of 12 percent is lethal.

Now, breathe.

Former Russian president Mikhail Gorbachev claims that we stand on the brink of a global water crisis, as all life everywhere is dependent upon water for survival, and we are polluting it rapidly.

We all know this: we know about droughts and floods, global warming, climate change, and attempts to privatize water. We know about the melting of the arctic glaciers and rising sea levels. We hopefully understand that bottling water solves nothing; in fact, it just adds more plastic to our oceans and landfills. So how do we start?

Watersheds

Brock Dolman,[2] director of the Water Institute at the Occidental Arts and Ecology Center in Northern California, says it simply. "Start at home. Start by knowing your watershed."

A watershed is the land area that drains into the local waterways, from high ground, where rain falls and runs into the local creeks, to the lowlands, where creeks enter the rivers, bays, or seas. I live near the divide of the Derby Creek and Temescal Creek watersheds, each creek system starting from springs in the East Bay hills which are then diverted into underground culverts, to empty into the San Francisco Bay.

Years ago, I learned about our bioregion's creeks from my irrepressible friend John Steere,[3] founder of the local Urban Creeks movement and head of the Green Planning Collaborative. One night in late summer, when the creek was merely a dribble, he took a few of us to the Temescal culvert, so that we could sing! Holding aloft burning candles to light our way, we slogged single file through the barely running creek into the booming darkness of the culvert. I will never forget that night: soaked sneakers and cold feet, the smells of creekwater and dripping hot wax, the camaraderie of our intrepid little band, then our voices echoing in this most amazingly resonant sound chamber.

That same year we all danced in the Earth Day parade, carrying aloft a 26-foot-long rainbow-colored fish. Cavorting down the avenue, flapping like a colorful dragon in the breeze, Ganish (Ganesh changed to rhyme with FISH) the Rainbow Fish was designed to symbolize Strawberry Creek, which ran just below our feet, invisible beneath the asphalt.

"It's right down here!" we chanted, pointing down at the roadway. "Right beneath us runs a creek!" Only now, almost 20 years later, is the city council finally seriously considering the proposal to bring our downtown creek into daylight for all to see and enjoy.

If it weren't for those places where the original creeks of our region come aboveground, most of us might never know they even exist. During heavy rains, the water overflows and floods our basements, to be pumped out by sump pumps and emptied back out into the streets to flow into storm drains, which of course are conduits for a lot more than water. Street trash gets picked up, along with oil and dead rodents, all of which gets dumped in the bay. This leaves a mess of tideline debris on the shores of the Bay, especially at my favorite cove.

Brock claims that our carelessness is a result of our not recognizing that we are community with everything in our watershed—"Basins of Relations," he calls it—from our fellow humans to the rock beneath our soil and the water that seeps through it. Our life cycle is entirely dependent upon all the cycles in our bioregion: trees and shrubs and grasses and every other living organism, from bacteria and insects to the raccoons and deer in our midst. Water cycles, and not knowing the geological history of the ground beneath our feet, nor all the living forms with whom we share our bioregion, is like not knowing our next-door neighbors. Which many of us do not. Perhaps it's time we went over and introduced ourselves.

Learning About Water Where You Live

Many communities have nature programs in ecology centers, schools, or churches that offer local watershed classes or films. Close to Home[4] is the name of one such program where I live in Berkeley. Held in the fellowship hall of a church once a month, invited speakers offer talks on such subjects as the geology of our region, the fate of monarch butterflies, and the raccoon population in our midst. I've learned about wild and cultivated bees, beavers, the deer proliferating in the hills, and the comeback of our previously endangered brown pelicans.

Programs like these are a wonderful opportunity for a family outing, not to mention a great time for the adults to learn about their own watersheds without admitting their ignorance to the children. In my town, there is even an annual Watershed Poetry Festival,[5] where local poets read to the assembled crowd and then we walk the trail along the creek together.

Creek restoration projects are happening in many communities. They are a wonderful way to spend a family afternoon, as are cleanup days at your local lake or river or ocean beach. If you looking for the perfect like-minded boyfriend or girlfriend, grab a bucket and head out to the beach on cleanup day! There is almost always a great picnic afterward, where you get to meet folks who care about the things you do.

With a little investigating, you may find that there are springs once sacred to the native peoples of your region not far from where you live. Many of these sites are no longer apparent, but some have been made into public parks or spas; a little research may reveal some interesting history right where you live. When we went searching, we turned up sites sacred to the Miwok peoples in the Bay Area and some hot springs a two-hour drive from home that I had never known were there.

If you live in the desert, take a hike out beyond town and notice how every dry feature of the land has been shaped, at one time or another, by water. And if you are interested in how water defines desert land, don't miss the work of Craig Childs,[6] my favorite of his books being *The Secret Knowledge of Water*.

Polluted Water

When I was young, the waters around New York City were polluted, and I took it as a fact of life that water was off-limits to kids. It did not occur to me then that it did not have to be that way. My secret dream, though, was to swim down a river, starting high in the mountains where a spring trickled out from some rocks, and float all the way to the sea. It is a fantasy I have never fulfilled, but recently I met a man who did—or at least, a man who followed one who did. Activist Christopher Swain swam the whole length of the Hudson River, with the filmmaker Tom Weidlinger[7] following him by boat with a camera, documenting the journey in a film entitled *Swim For the River*.

The filmmaker accomplished a feat almost as remarkable as the swimmer's: he brought the subject of water pollution to the attention of the viewer in such a way that we feel hope that we can address our problems rather than become helpless with despair. Tom's work, in fact, is part of my inspiration for writing this book.

When I mentioned my interest in water to a 14-year-old friend, he listened closely and then admitted, "I just turn on the tap and there's water—I guess I take it for granted." I think he is speaking for many of us, and I wonder why we have lost our intimacy with what our bodies are mostly composed of?

I remember women in India walking gracefully from the wells with pots of water balanced on their heads. I know they did not take for granted even one drop of that water. Nor do all the women in the world who have to walk for water. They have to walk farther now, as rivers are drying up, even the Nile, and the water table is sinking everywhere. In the American Southwest, the Navajo now have to fetch their water by truck from as far away as 10 miles from their homes.

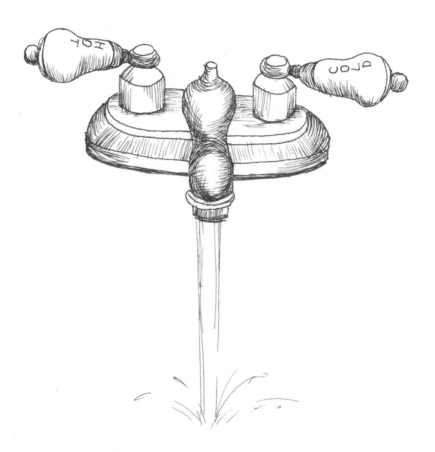

It has been suggested that our alienation from the natural world is partly due to the fact that most of us drink too little water and our bodies tend to be dehydrated, making us sluggish and tired. We have lost primal touch with our origins; instead, we keep ourselves lubricated with tea and coffee, sodas and juice, as we are encouraged to do by media advertisers. Coca-Cola, I recently learned, is so corrosive it will dissolve a nail in about four days and is used to remove rust and grease from engines. What must it do to a human stomach?

Does that make you thirsty? Writing that made me reach for my glass of water. Go ahead, take a drink—but not Coke, and not water that's in a nonrecyclable plastic bottle, please.

The Water Cycle

Historically, people chose to settle near bodies of water for all the obvious reasons. In modern times, however, technology has designed ways to pump, purify, and pipe water artificially, making it possible for people to live anywhere, even in the midst of deserts, and have water brought to them from afar. This, not surprisingly, has tended to deplete the aquifers of the originating ecosystems, which leads to a multitude of inevitable problems that, with a little bit of foresight, might have been predicted.

In the natural world, water cycles continuously from its gaseous form as it condenses off the ocean, transforms into clouds and mist that gather in the atmosphere, then falls as rain or snow. Rain droplets hit the earth and soak in, percolating down through roots and the fungal web, picking up nutrients and minerals before joining the flowing waters of a stream. In the cool, tree-shaded stream dappled by sunlight, this nutrient-rich water bubbles and swirls, spiraling and spraying as it tumbles around boulders and leaps over snags. It falls in thundering whitewater down rapids and waterfalls, gathers in lakes and glacial ice, gleams blue in deep crevasses.

Unlike the chemically purified water that comes through straight pipes to our faucets, out of reach of sunlight and starlight, this natural water has been "around the block;" it is water with experience. The Chinese refer to this water as "water that has gone up and down the mountain ten thousand times." If you have ever taken a drink from a mountain stream, you know the difference in taste between wild living water and tamed, chlorinated water from a tap.

As I write, it is raining—the first rain of the season. Stepping outside, I watch fat drops pelt the dry ground of the garden, seeping in and disappearing out of sight to become groundwater. The rain infiltrates the ground slowly and becomes recharged in its percolating journey through soil and rock, through roots of plants and bacteria and fungi, and eventually into streams and rivers. Where the pavement starts beyond the garden, however, the water begins to puddle, having no way in, and where there's a slight decline in the sidewalk the drops gather and make a small rivulet that runs downhill, over concrete, toward the storm drain. The earth will never see that water.

Engineers have designed our streets to do just that—to get the water running off paved surfaces as quickly as possible—even though Nature has designed the porous soil to do just the opposite: to receive the rain, pick up nutrients, and replenish the groundwater. Pavement runoff, however, also picks up the toxins on our streets, carrying them to the storm drains to be flushed out to sea with the rainwater.

So here's the dilemma: in our cities, with their sidewalks and asphalt roadways, rainwater pools and, in heavy rain, probably floods if it does not run off; but the earth and its plants and animals—which includes us humans—need that same rain to replenish its groundwater. We've got a conflict of interest here! What do we do?

Catch It, Slow It, Spread It, Sink It

"Catch it and then release it slowly," says my friend, the artist and plumber Christina Bertea, matter-of-factly. "SLOW IT, SPREAD IT, SINK IT is the mantra for water," she adds.

I first met Christina, a passionate advocate for water, when she crawled under our kitchen sink to struggle with a rusted pipe. After finishing the job, she emerged filthy and smiling like a rosy-cheeked cherub. She produced her invoice on the back of a postcard picturing the sculpture of a woman with face lifted to the rain and hands cupped to catch it. It was world-class art, and I asked her where it came from. Her shy blush told me it was her own, and when I asked to see more, she invited me to her house and studio. We've been friends ever since.

This amazing woman has also dreamed up a rainwater rattle, made of an old copper toilet ball, that looks like an ancient artifact and sounds like one, too. She has designed a gorgeous rain catchment sculpture that is shaped like a giant daisy. Funneling falling rain into a 55-gallon barrel, the flower's outspread petals are shaped with a pair of tin snips, cut from a roll of sheet metal, and *ping* satisfyingly when the raindrops hit them. Because of the petals, this catchment barrel can be freestanding and does not need to be placed below a downspout from the roof. Rain catchment barrels are also designed to be placed below downspouts, and are often available from your city for a discount.

Large-size garbage cans, wine barrels, even buckets from the hardware store can be used just as well. Christina has added the whimsy of curly floral pistils in the center, made from a thrift-store wire whisk with glass baubles on the tips! With a little imagination and a spirit of can-do, you can create your own flower, or upturned umbrella to catch the rain. A barrel, some stiff, impermeable material, and a cutter is all you need.

In the interest of providing more places for rain to soak into the earth, my neighbor Ken Smith has pried up his cement driveway and replaced it with gravel, through which raindrops can percolate and infiltrate the soil. (*Slow it, spread it, sink it.*) The hunks of concrete then became "urbanite" rocks in his beautiful native rock garden—a straightforward switcheroo!

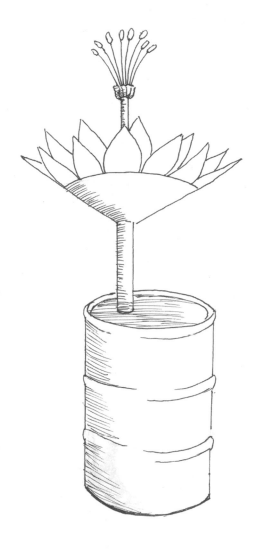

A rain-friendly driveway can also be made with permeable bricks or paving stones, now readily available in plant nurseries, which can be mixed and matched in any design you wish. In my own dream driveway, I would find used tiles and pavers of many colors at our local recycling place, Urban Ore, out of which I would fashion a many-colored mosaic, and between the pavers I would plant creeping thyme and chamomile so that every time you pulled into the driveway the scent of crushed herb would fill the air. I've been imagining this for years, and no doubt will do it one day—as soon as my husband lets me take a sledgehammer to the driveway...

If you live in a place where outdoor space is limited or not your own—as in a rental unit or an apartment house—you might try putting a few small buckets, clean ones, on the windowsills or fire escape and catch the rain when it pours. Even a little bit is enough to wash your hair in, or water your houseplants. You might even use it to cook up the pasta, soak your beans, or make a soup—for a soup, do filter it first. Amaze your friends and family with rainwater soup!

I hear Christina adding, "Tell them that when they drain the spaghetti, they should catch the water and feed the plants with it, too!"

Water All Around You

West Marrin,[8] water scientist and author of *Universal Water*, is a wonderful man who claims that the best way to understand water and its place in our lives is to be *in* it. He lives near the sea, swims daily, and surfs whenever the wind is up. Most of us don't live at the shore, but we might follow his suggestion anyway and wash our children (and ourselves, if there is enough of it) in gently warmed rainwater. The more of us imprinted with the feel and quality of natural, rather than treated water on our bodies when we are small, the more of us who will have an innate awareness of our connection to water as we grow, as people who live close to the earth do.

Living as I do in a bioregion that is dry for much of the year, my family has created a fountain in one corner of the garden by digging out a miniature pond-bed, filling it with water, and surrounding the pond with driftwood and stones gathered from around San Francisco Bay. It refills itself during the rainy season, and during the dry times we replenish it with first-run water from our shower. For me, as for many people living in dry climes, the sound of running water nearby is essential when the rainless months go on and on. In our self-designed fountain, water falls into the pool from the top of an upended driftwood log Christina and I found while beachcombing one day, and spills across the roots to tumble into the pool. Leaves and plum blossoms drift onto the pool, depending upon the season, making it look even more like a natural grotto. I love watching the neighborhood wildlife—cats, hummingbirds, squirrels— use it as their watering hole.

Another use for captured rainwater is to fill a bird bath. Jeanne Pimentel has placed hers right outside her kitchen window, where she can watch the local wildlife flit in and out, splashing happily in the rare waterhole. As long as the birds splash, mosquito larvae will not settle, but if you find them, a daily scoop-out with a kitchen strainer will catch them before they hatch. For a larger pond, try adding mosquito fish. Mosquitoes prefer standing water to lay their eggs in, so keep it moving!

Rain in the Garden

Rainwater is mainly caught directly in the garden, of course, and if you landscape with native plants, the normal rain pattern of your region will supply most of the water you need.

My neighbor Alex Nowik, who loves the plants of this area, has created a native prairie in his yard. He started it with seeds gathered from our hillsides: fennel and yarrow, sticky monkeyflower and cow parsnip, and his garden is now its own native ecosystem, the grasses and shrubs and flowers buzzing with bees and butterflies and flitting birds. He rarely has to water and has the best time with his bit of wildness. I always stop to admire it when I pass by, and when he is about, I compliment him on his handiwork. "Nature's handiwork," he corrects me with a smile, offering me cow parsnip seeds in the fall, or clumps of feathery yarrow plants for my garden.

People are making roof gardens these days, mostly using containers, but some are making living roofs by putting down soil and planting directly onto membranes that cover the surface of the reinforced roof. Water-catchment barrels strategically placed can water the roof or redistribute rainwater directly into the building as graywater for flushing toilets or watering the indoor greenery. Perhaps these roof gardens are a New World equivalent of the ancient hanging gardens of Babylon. In Chicago, City Hall[9] has a miniature prairie growing on its roof, and in San Francisco, the new Academy of Sciences[10] building sports a whole native ecosystem on its roof, both open to the public.

One of our local hospitals has installed a small healing garden on an outdoor porch, where small trees and fragrant shrubs grow in containers. Patients may come out, wheeling their rolling I.V. poles, to sit in the sun surrounded by green growing things, and visitors may wait there for their loved ones in a much more calming atmosphere than a fluorescent-lit waiting room. Visiting a friend at the hospital recently, I watched mesmerized as a Chinese gentleman did a slow, dance-like prayer in front of a potted magnolia tree the whole time his wife was in surgery. Watching him, I think I understood, perhaps for the first time, how essential it is for us to be in reciprocal relationship with the natural world. I also got it that we, and the trees in our midst, are natural allies, if for no other reason than that trees bring rain.

The Forest is the Mother of Water

"The forest is the mother of water," writes Richard St. Barbe Baker.[11] Cut down the trees, and the organic leaf-fall that acts like a sponge—the natural flood control layer—vanishes. As we humans clear-cut forests and alter the flow of water, we affect weather patterns, which in turn affects all life on Earth. I marvel that the lumber industry ignores the connection. As Barbara Kingsolver recently put it, "Water is the visible face of climate, and therefore, climate change." Currently, the planet is experiencing thousands of violent storms, floods, and tornadoes as a result. Brook Jensen, a young arborist I know, says everybody should be planting a tree a day, and I believe her.

In Peru, on foggy, desertified hillsides that once were dense forest, people have set huge, multilayered plastic mesh nets to catch the fog. Once caught, it condenses into droplets that are funneled into pipes that then drain into underground cisterns. People are now replanting trees, and with the tens of thousands of gallons of moisture captured each year, they are nourishing newly planted trees that they hope will restore the forest.

In desert areas, where rain is sporadic and mostly runs off, hand-built swales are being used to harvest water, prevent erosion, and grow trees for shade. This can be done on a smaller scale in our urban gardens as well. A swale is a trough or ditch dug on the contour of your land, where the removed soil forms a berm along the downhill side. The berm then effectively stops and catches the rainwater that would otherwise flow away, and holds it in the swale, like a canal of water, to soak in. Then you plant trees right into the berms where the tree roots can access the water year round. In cities, too, especially Portland, Oregon, and Seattle in the Pacific Northwest, a permaculture movement is afoot to place swales between houses in neighborhoods to capture rainwater.

Catch it, slow it, spread it, sink it.

One permaculture method is to plant fast-growing pioneer trees along newly dug swales, fixing nitrogen into the soil. As they drop their leaves, they mulch their own roots and fertilize the soil, which in turn, holds moisture more effectively. As the soil becomes fertile, other food crops—roots, vines, shrubs, even fruiting trees—can be planted among them. Swales are the first step in the storage of water in the landscape itself, and of reclaiming land that has been damaged, denuded, eroded, desertified. May they prosper!

Graywater

West Marrin is the person who convinced me that our water crisis is the result of our misuse of water, not that there is less water on the planet. The current volume of water is the same as it has been since the beginning of time, but a large percentage of it has been rendered useless to life because we have mindlessly polluted it. We have a million ways of dirtying it, too few ways of cleaning it, then we send it down the drain.

At our house, we once used freshwater to bathe, do laundry, flush our toilets, and wash the dishes, mostly not noticing it disappear down the drain and out of sight—that is, until I started writing this book. Much of this water—with the exception of toilet water—is called "greywater" and is commonly considered to be contaminated and dangerous. In fact, most of it is not. Greywater comprises half to three-quarters of household wastewater, contains no pollutants if you use nontoxic soaps and detergents, and is safe for the irrigation of trees, bushes, shrubs, and flowers. We are asked not to water root crops with it, or allow it to touch the edible parts of plants, but used with care, it is perfectly benign.

Toilet flushing accounts for a large percentage of daily household water use, and for reasons I have never understood, our toilets flush clean drinking-quality water down with every flush. As population grows all around the world and people covet a Western standard of living, we could find ourselves collectively flushing whatever remains of the world's freshwater right down the toilet. It makes as little sense as cutting down virgin forests to make paper napkins—or toilet paper, for that matter.

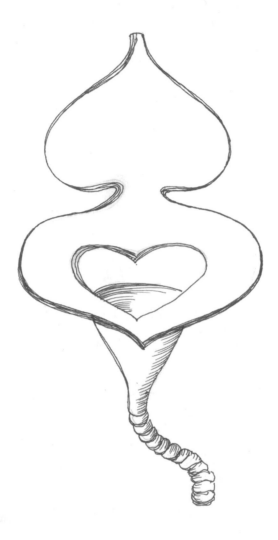

Christina has designed a prototype of a urine-separating compost toilet seat shaped like a heart, to whimsically propose that we might harvest our own urine. She reminded me that urine, diluted with 3-to-10 parts water, is a perfect nitrogen fertilizer for the garden. There are a variety of methods for capturing our urine, most fairly easy to do once we get used to the idea. I have a friend, good citizen that he is, who pees into his compost pile every night before bedtime. In England, the men tending the gardens at the stately homes run by the National Trust are required to urinate in stacks of straw bales when they have to "go," which eventually become mulch in the gardens. As Christina has said, "We, too, are part of the earth's nutrient cycle."

Pee-Pee Ponics

Like nitrogen, phosphorus is an essential element for growing food; unlike nitrogen, phosphorus is only found in rock—rapidly being strip-mined into extinction for the commercial fertilizer industry—and in urine. As more and more urine gets flushed down the toilet and natural rock sources are mined to depletion, we will find ourselves in a situation Christina calls "Peak Phosphorus."

Pee-pee ponics is concerned with harvesting rather than flushing away our urine. Ecological designer Nik Bertulis[12] has created an inspired Pee-Pee Ponic garden in a box made out of scrap wood, a funnel, and layers of soil and compost. Using wooden pallets lined with a permeable liner, he has filled about two-thirds of the box with a fluffy "carbon" layer of straw, wood chips, dry leaves, and cardboard. The top third of the box is filled with humus-rich soil, into which is planted leafy, nitrogen-loving green vegetables: spinach, kale, lettuce.

A wide-mouthed funnel, for peeing directly into, is placed on the outside of the box about halfway up the "carbon" layer, its flexible pipe extending into the middle of the box where urine deposits (due to the design, it is mainly aimed at use by men) create a nitrogen and phosphorus-rich stream. The nutrient and phosphorus-filled urine then soaks into the compost layer and is wicked up into the soil layer by osmosis, allowing it to water and brings essential nutrients to the roots of the plants growing there. The urine itself never touches the greens, the humus in the soil neutralizes any ammonia odor of the urine, the plants rarely need other watering, and within a year the carbon layer is gorgeous compost that may be recycled into the rest of the garden and replaced with fresh straw, wood chips, and leaves.

Flush Variations

I once spent a week alone at a friend's forest cabin in Vermont. The water pump broke on the day I was leaving, so there was no running water in the cabin. I had a plane to catch but was not willing to leave without flushing the toilet so, not knowing what else to do, I took every bottle of soda water, beer, and wine I could find in the kitchen and tossed their contents down the toilet to activate the flushing mechanism. I recall adding a can of tomato juice for good measure. It worked like a charm.

Christina has strong opinions about toilets. She speaks rapturously of her current favorite: the "Ultra High Efficiency" toilet from Hennessy and Hinchcliffe[13] in Ontario, Canada. She cajoled Herb and me into installing one in our house because it uses only three liters or .8 of a gallon of water per full flush and she wanted someone in the community to demonstrate it to start the ball rolling. Three liters per flush is substantially less than the new 1.28-gallon standard requirement, and what makes the difference, Christina tells me, is that pressure is maintained in the trapway instead of in the tank. It works! You are welcome to come over to try it out, but by the time this book is published I expect it will be all the rage everywhere.

Easy Does it With Gray

When we use ecologically responsible soaps and detergents without sodium or boron, the graywater that comes from our bathing and laundry are benign enough to go directly into either the garden outdoors or into potted plants growing indoors. Short of more complicated systems that require plumbing and three-way valves, here are some easy ideas anybody can follow:

- Place a plastic tub or bucket in your bathroom sink to catch your face-washing, teeth-brushing, and hand-washing water, and flush your toilet with it. A filled bathroom sink–size basin is the perfect volume for a single flush.
- Have a bucket handy by the shower to catch the first cold water that runs before the water heats up. This water is perfectly clean. I save it for our outdoor fountain, the vegetables in the garden, and washing out underwear. Sometimes I pour it out a second-story window onto my climbing rose in the garden below. This gets a rise out of the neighbors!
- If you wash dishes by hand, as I do, place a plastic tub in the kitchen sink, and have a bucket on the floor ready for pouring used dishwashing water. Be sure your dish soap contains neither boron nor sodium. Since this water has food particles in it, it is one step dirtier than official greywater from the shower or laundry. It can be used in the garden but must be poured into mulched areas—such as around the base of fruit trees—where the water will neither run off nor pool on the surface. I use it mostly on our thirsty roses.
- OK, so where's the fun in all this? It's a game I play: I go out with my bucket when I'm in the mood for company. People always stop and chat when I'm out in the garden, so I empty out water buckets when I hear neighbors out on the street and am glad to spend a bit of time catching up on everyone's news.
- My friend Melissa Prager brings her houseplants into the shower with her when she and they need to be watered and puts them both on a timer. I dub this technology Showers into Flowers.
- Of course, there are more technical ways of moving greywater from the house to your garden, and as these technologies are rapidly becoming accepted in the plumbing codes, this information will be more and more available from

your local plumbers. Right now, in Berkeley where greywater plumbing has recently become legal, you can hardly find a seat when one of the Greywater Guerillas[14] is speaking in town.

Moving greywater from house to garden implies, of course, that you have a house and a garden. For those who do not, it is still feasible to use the greywater you catch in your sinks for watering houseplants, flushing the toilet, or bathing the dog. Why use clean water to scrub the tub? Or wash the car? Or mop the kitchen floor?

If you do have a garden, the easiest greywater source to start with is the washing machine because its plumbing is relatively uncomplicated. You simply run the drain hose from the washing machine to a barrel outside and nearby, and another hose from the barrel directly into the garden. The hose will drain by gravity, so you need a bit of a slope, if possible. Remember to move the hose regularly so that the water reaches all your plants and does not pool on the surface of the ground.

More complicated greywater systems should be done carefully and professionally. Water-loving plants can be planted where puddles tend to form, and you might enhance these low spots by encouraging rainwater to flow there even more. Then search the nurseries to find plants that thrive with their roots in water.

Another idea is to find a discarded old sink or bathtub, haul it back to your house, and dig it into the ground, preferably near a rainspout, to create a pond for water plants. (Remember to keep it skimmed of mosquito larvae.) This is the kind of deep play I really enjoy; it takes nerve and a whole village to pull off, not to mention a stout pickup truck for transporting the tub; don't try it alone.

So, with some imagination and a spirit of fun, can we help recycle our precious water back into the earth's water table?

YES WE CAN!

When can we do it?

NOW!

Can every one of us do it in some fairly simple ways at home?

YOU BETCHA!

Deep Play

Deep play and a passionate commitment to water motivates my friend Sharon Pavelda. Her mission is to wake people up with humor. She goes out onto the streets wildly costumed, calling her gig "an opening act for God." Her character Wa-wa is decked out in a gazillion plastic water bottles. Sharon takes her to churches, seminaries, schools, the streets, the beach—wherever people gather.

"I want to take people back to their undefended childhood imaginations," she says, "and stimulate them to do what they already want to do. Water takes us back to the deep connection that we are all yearning for, because we are essentially made of water ourselves."

While we were talking she was interrupted by a call on her "shell-phone" from Mother Ganga, reminding us that the sacred river was in trouble and needed our prayers. Before parting ways, she gave me a slippery hug, no mean feat if one of you is covered with plastic water bottles!

Although I wish plastic bottles had never been invented, since they are here and everywhere, one way of keeping them out of the gyres of plastic trash in our oceans is to make things with them: sun-catching mobiles, sea-going boats, and a wonderful toy that uses two bottles that create a swirling vortex between them. Starting with two undented, two-liter soda bottles, some water, and a two-inch piece of one/half diameter plastic pipe, you can create your own miniature whirlpool, or twister, and watch it vortex for hours. Joining the water-filled bottles at their mouths with the PVC pipe tightly inserted between them, you give the water a quick swirl to get it started, and for the next hour watch mesmerized as it spins and spins in a perfect vortex, just like a miniature typhoon.[15]

In July 2003, Cynthia Winton-Henry, who with Phil Porter founded the Interplay[16] community of dancers and activists, invited everybody to celebrate Earth Day at the Port of Oakland, dancing and singing for the health of water, where the waters of the bay and the industrial world intersect. It was potent prayer. Interplay is all about deep play, social activism, faith, and creativity, and Cynthia is one of the most remarkable movers and shakers we have.

Betsy Damon[17] is called a conceptual humanist and artist; to me, she is one of the great hands-on visionaries in the world today. What she has achieved in the spirit of deep play I would have considered impossible, but she's done it. On the banks of the Yangtze River in Chengdu, Sichuan Province in China, she has created, with a team of visionaries like herself, the world's first municipal living-water garden. The idea was to make a Living Water Park out of the polluted river flowing by the city, by designing forms through which the water would pass in new ways: filtering reed beds, vortical flowforms, and sculptures that would aerate the water by keeping it flowing the way a healthy, natural watercourse flows. Her idea was to restore the river to a high level of health, which would also affect the larger ecosystem of the Chengdu region through "subtle, alive, complex, life-giving, freely-flowing water." Vibrant with oxygen, the river would be better able to resist pollution. Her claim was that if we cleaned up the world's water, especially in playful and imaginative ways, we would probably clean up 95 percent of our diseases as well.

The Living Water Park has pools and climbing rocks, walkways and flowing brooks, fountains and shallow ponds for the people of Chengdu to play in. It is a masterwork of public art for the betterment of all beings, an exquisite expression of art as a political act and a wonderful park for people of all ages to play in. It is a sacred water site, which interestingly was what she had originally come to China to study.

The Mystery of Water

We know that water goes through transitions from gas to liquid to solid, but science has never been able to explain exactly how. The fact is that nobody really understands the structure of water, nor has anybody ever actually seen a water molecule.

Galileo said:

> *I had fewer difficulties discovering the motions of the heavenly bodies, despite their incredible distances than I did investigating the motion of flowing water, which takes place right before our eyes.*

And a more contemporary version from West Marrin:

> *The journey from water, the element, to the H2O molecule is just the prelude to water's mystery. It is a journey that is not about water alone, but about our whole concept of the material world.*

My own feeling is that by neither recognizing the mystery nor acknowledging how little we actually know about water, we have mistakenly treated it as commonplace. "Too proud to write ourselves into text books along with clouds, rivers, and morning dew," says Craig Childs, "we find ourselves floundering, not knowing, as a species, how to swim in a watery world."

Ancient and indigenous cultures considered water to be sacred because it was a link to the Divine, a living, conscious entity that gave rise to the material world. The primordial ocean, according to creation stories from around the world, was the Source from which our whole world emerged out of nothingness.

According to the Maori of New Zealand, water has memory and remembers its journeys among the stars before seeping into many crevices of the earth's body. The Kogi people of Colombia use the same word for water as they use for spirit; they believe that their people were created by "water thinking" and, therefore, venerate water.

Ethnographer Wade Davis writes that the Indians of Vaupes in Colombia consider rivers to be "not just routes of communication, they are the veins of the earth, the link between the living and the dead, the paths along which the ancestors traveled since the beginning of time."

Theodor Schwenk has said it this way:

> *Water occupies a median position between Earth and the Universe and is the port of entry through which cosmic-peripheral forces pass into the earth realm ...*

And West Marrin, this way:

> *The ancient truism that water serves as a mediator in our world seems to be valid on both macrocosmic and microscopic scales.*

But only by a subjective experience of the subtle, mysterious nature of water will any of these words make sense to most of us.

I once got hopelessly lost in the woods and had no idea how to find my way back to the road. Earlier, I had forded a small brook, so I thought that if I could find my way back to the brook, I could follow it back to familiar terrain. But how to find the brook? Then some instinct told me to smell for it. I began slowly turning in place, got very quiet, and sniffed first in one direction, then the next, until I sensed some difference in the air, very faint but noticeable. My body registered it as water, and I took a chance and struck out in that direction, until I indeed found the brook and my way back.

It made a big impression on me, once I had stopped trembling and had something to eat, because I realized I had called upon a deep, subtle sense rarely employed, that had helped me find my way back. It was like hearing overtones when listening very quietly to the strike of a bell—or sensing the presence of someone not yet seen. I was deeply impressed. I have been stalking the subtle beast ever since, witnessing the elusive movements of water and using them as my model and metaphor for the invisible motions of subtle energy.

Holy Water

Growing up Jewish, I was always fascinated by the font of holy water near the portals in churches. If I dipped my fingers in, what would happen? Would I suddenly see God?

When holy water from a font is analyzed, after having been used prayerfully by many people, its chemical structure is changed from the structure of the original tap water it came from. Leaving aside for a moment the oils and bacteria on people's fingers that are present, it is as if water has the ability to register impressions from the people dipping into it and seems to be energetically charged by their prayerful intentions. Or as the Maori say: it has memory.

Japanese water researcher and chairman of the International HADO organization, Dr. Masuro Emoto,[18] author of *The Hidden Messages in Water*, has experimented with sending thoughts to water—kind thoughts and mean thoughts—before freezing it to the crystal stage and taking its micro-photograph through a high-powered lens. He has discovered that complimented crystals are symmetrical and beautiful while cursed crystals are dark and unformed.

Sandra Ingerman,[19] who trains people in shamanic techniques collaborates with scientist and psychoenergetics researcher Dr. William Tiller.[20] Together they have visualized, drummed, and chanted healing intentions into water, and find the water affected in subtle and positive ways. They are interested in discovering if groups of people chanting and drumming, with the intention of turning polluted water back into clean water, can in fact do so. Healers through the ages have chanted to affect people's bodies, which are mostly water, so it is logical to consider that water may indeed be affected by prayer and sound. If so, then perhaps we have more power than we thought to help heal ourselves and our polluted waters.

Tuning to Water

The philosopher and teacher Rudolph Steiner wrote about the old "clay singers" in Bavaria. Each spring, these farmers would fill barrels with water in which was dissolved a preparation of cow manure that had overwintered in their fields, stuffed into cow horns! (The more outrageous this gets, the better I like it.) Then they stirred the water first in one direction, then in the other, singing the whole time. They would do this for hours, stirring and singing—up the scale when stirring to the right, down the scale when stirring to the left. At each reversal of direction, the water churned into a bubbling chaos, much as it does in a running stream. The chaos of bubbles was when the magic was supposed to happen.

After sprinkling this charged water onto their fields—water charged with stirred vortices, the vibrations of their sounds, and their intentions for a good harvest—the fields invariably produced higher yields than those of neighboring farms.

I am reminded of how it feels to walk the path of a labyrinth, twisting right, then left, then right, then left. I wonder if I am not stirring the water in my body into vortices the way those farmers stirred the water in their barrels. After all, being made mostly of water, it would spiral back and forth in us, as it does everywhere in Nature. The spiral is the pattern of the solar system itself, as well as the galaxies. I wonder if the spiral might be the very motion that mediates between the invisible realms and the earthly realms, with water as the primary go-between? In any case, after I've traced the round-and-round pattern in the labyrinth, I feel remarkably clear and balanced, centered and calm.

The mystery seems to be right here in a million ways, hidden in plain sight if only we can learn how to look. The Chinese sages pointed the way, telling us to watch the water that goes up and down the mountain 10,000 times—the living water, the water with memory, the water that connects us with the Divine. It is holy water, not to be misused.

My friend John—the one I argued with on the winter beach long ago—died recently. He phoned me shortly before his death to say goodbye and to thank me for our time together. We talked tenderly of the past and the sad fact that we probably could not have made a life with each other.

"You're still the ardent idealist, aren't you?" he observed, in his slightly sarcastic tone, still so familiar after all these years. It was probably the reason I never could have married him.

"I guess I am," I sighed. "Maybe it's because I still love the mystery of the ocean." We both laughed softly, then I got up the nerve to add, only half in jest, "I think you may soon be in touch with the mystery, too." He surprised me by replying: "Yes, I know. When I am, I'll let you know."

I told him I loved him and for the first time, I genuinely meant it.

Water may flow in a thousand channels,
but it all returns to the sea.
—*AFRICAN PROVERB*

ADDITIONAL INSPIRATIONS

Invocation to the Ocean was created by Eilish Nagel for a gathering of her own tribe, and has been offered to all who might wish to use it for their own tribes.

Welcome, all, dancers and dolphins.
Welcome, mermaids and monsters,
You crafty sponges, you wily plankton.
As we enter the current here, close your eyes
And feel the ocean inside you ...
You are 70 percent seawater, you can taste it in the salt lick
Of your sweet summer sweat.
You are Yemayah,
And you are the child floating on her great belly.

As we hear the rhythm of this breath, this bloodstream,
Let your body find its sway, moving back and forth with current,
With tide, with whirlpools of everything that is here.
Ocean turns nothing away.

Feel the first time you felt sea on your skin,
The last time you dove in,

Feel the first time you got tumbled by a wave,
Snatched by a sleeper and taken, surprise riptide,
Further than you thought you could ever go.
This wave, the silly sandcastles you have built
And seen wash away, and returned the next day.
Turn none of it away.

Ocean holds every movement, every thought,
Every prayer,
Pulls it deep into her belly
And offers it back to us in the next wave,
Saying, "Here."

This is the gratitude for every drop.
This is the forgiveness for every drop not felt.
You have been surfed and cherished and worshipped,
And you have been drilled and bled.
This is for the waters running red.

This wave for those in reverence,
This wave for those in greed,
And every deed that leaves either
Altar or a tar ball on your shore.

This wave, a school of healers
reknitting your torn ocean floor.

This wave connects us all—
We are not drops, but ocean,
Our currents weaving together.
So in the swing of your sway,
The sweet curl of your crest,
Let yourself be celebration,
Dance with play, or pray,
Whatever moves you, your own way.
This wave, surfers, this wave,
Every jewel left at your feet by the low tide,
This wave, every jewel caught
By casting your intention out and reeling in your life.

This wave, all of us, our swirling, swimming tribe,
Those here and those not,
The children who are swimming elsewhere today,
The families who couldn't come,
The friends who have passed:
Call them into these waters,
Because each of you is on your way somewhere.
So as we meet the different faces of ocean
we meet ourselves too:
calm, and stormy, clear and murky
turn none of it away
we bless us all today.

Pee-Pee Ponics' motto is: There can never be too much funny in the green movement. For more information, visit *www.youtube.com/watch?v=vK-16SFV4lI*

Diane Ackerman is a poet, essayist, and naturalist. She is the author of two dozen works of nonfiction and poetry, (See the chapter "Water, Water Everywhere" in the recently published *Dawn Light: Dancing with Cranes, and other ways to Start the Day* (Norton 2009) For more information, visit *http://dianeackerman.com/works.htm*

The Wild Swim Movement in the United Kingdom encourages people to find hidden, wild waterways and to jump in! For more information visit *www.wildswimming. co.uk*

Rain Thanks consults, designs, and installs regenerative water systems and strategies that are simple, affordable, and efficient. Their systems are designed to reduce irrigation/water cost while creating a vibrant, healthy and edible landscape tailored to each site. For more information, visit *www.rainthanks.com*

Green Visions was an internet radio show I hosted in 2010 consisting of 13 interviews on the Voice America Internet Radio. Three of the interviews are on the subject of water. To listen online, visit *www.healingimprovisations.net/audio/radio/*

Colorado Water Law: There is a strange water law in the state of Colorado based on a principle known as "First in time, first in right." This was set up about 150 years ago by farmers and ranchers, who claimed "ownership of the rain!" As a result, it is still illegal there to catch and store your own roof water, or any of its runoff. Even if your house is located on the river itself, to take a bucket of its water is considered a crime. I've never been to Colorado, but I do hope my friends there are disobedient rascals.

This is from Leonardo da Vinci:

> *Water is sometimes sharp and sometimes strong, sometimes acid and sometimes bitter, sometimes sweet and sometimes thick or thin, sometimes it brings hurt or pestilence, sometimes it is health- giving, sometimes poisonous. It can change into as many forms as the different places through which it passes. As the mirror changes with the color of its object, so water alters with the nature of the place, becoming noisome, laxative, astringent, sulfurous, salt, bloody, mournful, raging, angry, red, yellow, green, black, blue, greasy, fat or slim. Sometimes it starts fires and sometimes it extinguishes them;*

sometimes is warm, sometimes cold. Sometimes it carries things away, sometimes sets them down, hollows out or builds up, tears down or creates, fills or empties, raises itself or burrows down, speeds or is still. Sometimes it causes life, sometimes death; sometimes increase or privation; sometimes it nourishes and sometimes does not; sometimes has taste and sometimes is without savor. And sometimes it covers the land with great floods. With water, in time, everything changes.

ENDNOTES

1. **Theodor Schwenk** (1910–1986) was an anthroposophist, an engineer, and pioneering water researcher who founded the Institute for Flow Science. To Schwenk, cosmic consciousness was symbolized by water, where all particles merged into a single, transcendental entity. For more information visit *en.wikipedia.org/wiki/Theodor-Schwenk*

2. **Brock Dolman** is director of the Water Institute at the Occidental Arts and Ecology Center in Northern California. He also directs OAEC's Permaculture Program, co-directs the center's Wildlands Biodiversity Program, and co-manages its biodiversity collection, orchards, and 70 acres of wildlands. By nature a "specialized generalist," Dolman's interests are wide ranging and include wildlife biology, native California botany, and watershed ecology, as well as habitat restoration, educating the public about regenerative human settlement design, ethnoecology, and ecological literacy activism toward societal transformation. For more information, visit *www.oaecwater.org/brock-dolman-bio*

3. **John Steere** is an environmental planner with experience managing collaborative environmental, land use, and resource management plans and programs throughout California He is the founder of East Bay Citizens for Creek Restoration and a former board director of both the Occidental Arts and Ecology Center and Urban Creeks Council He has led a number of creek revegetation projects in the East Bay and co-led the planning and installation of a community-based park that now occupies a converted parking lot in Berkeley. For more information, visit *www.facebook.com/john.steere*

4. **Close to Home** is an environmental education forum that provides speakers for monthly talks in the San Francisco Bay Area that help people access the natural world of the East Bay. The focus of the forum is living with wildlife. For more information, visit *http://baynature.org/organizations/close-to-home*

5. The **Watershed Poetry Festival** is a free day of poetry, music, and activism that explores the state of the planet. It hosts numerous writers, from youth poets to environmental speakers. For more information, visit *http://baynature.org/events/watershed-environmental-poetry-festival/?searchterm=poetry*

6. **Craig Childs** is a writer/adventurer based in Colorado who focuses on natural sciences, archaeology, and mind-blowing journeys into the wilderness. He has published more than a dozen critically acclaimed books on Nature, science, and adventure. His subjects range from pre-Columbian archaeology to U.S. border issues to the last free-flowing rivers of Tibet. The expeditions Childs undertake

often last weeks or months, informing his writing with a hard-earned sense of landscape and culture. For more information, visit *www.houseofrain.com/ theauthor.cfm*

7. **Tom Weidlinger** is an independent filmmaker who has been writing, directing, and producing documentary films for 28 years. Sixteen of his films have been broadcast nationally on public television. Weidlinger's work deals with a wide range of subjects, from the emotional development of boys in the United States to humanitarian aid in the Congo. The themes of social justice and human relations run through his films. For more information, visit *www.swimfortheriver. com* or *www.moiraproductions.com*

8. **West Marrin** is dedicated to providing people with intellectual and experiential tools for reassessing their perceptions of water. West's most recent e-book, *Hydromimicry*, portrays water as a model for approaching global challenges. For more information, visit *www.watersciences.org*

9. **The Roof Gardens at Chicago City Hall** were completed in 2001 as a prototype to test what impact green roofs would have on the "heat island" effect in urban areas, rainwater runoff, and the effectiveness of differing types of green roofs and plant species for Chicago's climate. Noted green architect William McDonough designed the project. For more information, visit *http://www.asla.org/meetings/ awards/awds02/chicagocityhall.html*

10. **The Living Roof at the Academy of Sciences** in Golden Gate Park, San Francisco, is a 197,000-square-foot rooftop that was built to accommodate a living tapestry of native plant species A total of 50,000 porous, biodegradable trays made from tree sap and coconut husks were used as containers for the vegetation. The Living Roof´s 1.7 million native plants were specially chosen to flourish in Golden Gate Park´s climate. For more information, visit *http://www.calacademy.org/academy/building/the_living_roof.php*

11. **Richard St. Barbe Baker** (1889–1982) was an English forester, environmental activist, and author who contributed greatly to worldwide reforestation efforts. As a leader, he founded an organization, still active today, whose many chapters carry out reforestation internationally. For more information, visit *www. manofthetrees.org*

12. **Nik Bertulis** describes himself as an amateur naturalist and a professional water nerd. For more information, visit *www. nikbertulis.com*

13. **Hennessy and Hinchcliffe Inc.** launched the world's first 3.0 litre-per-flush high-efficiency toilet in 2009. The current model, the H & H N7716, is a toilet designed in Canada that features revolutionary flushing technology and superior performance. Developed by the same design team behind the Niagara Flapper-

less leak-free toilet, the H & H N7716 is promoted as the world's most efficient single-flush toilet, cutting domestic water consumption in half. For more information, visit *http://www.watermatrix.com/mediaroom_3.0.php*

14. **Greywater Action** and **Greywater Guerillas** provide educational workshops and resources for greywater reuse, rainwater harvesting, and composting toilets in the San Francisco Bay Area. For more information, visit *www.greywateraction.org*

15. **Water Vortex Game** is made with two plastic water bottles placed mouth to mouth. For assembly instructions please visit *www.sciencetoymaker.org/vortex/assembl.html.*

16. **InterPlay** is easy and fun and teaches the language and ethic of play in a deep way. It is based on a series of incremental "forms" that lead participants to movement and stories, silence and song, ease and amusement, thereby unlocking the wisdom of their bodies and the wisdom in their communities. For more information, visit *www.interplay.org*

17. **Keepers of the Waters** has as its stated mission the goal of inspiring and promoting projects that combine art, science, and community involvement to restore, preserve, and remediate water sources. Founder Betsy Damon says: "Water is the foundation of life, the connective might of the Universe; therefore, sustaining the water systems must be the foundation of planning and development." For more information, visit *www.keepersofthewaters.org*

18. **Masuru Emoto** is a Japanese author and water researcher who has photographed ice crystals as they are spoken to with either love or distaste, and discovered that the crystals respond appropriately. Several photo books of his work have been published. For more information, visit *www.masaru-emoto.net*

19. **Sandra Ingerman** teaches soul retrieval, shamanism, healing, and reversing environmental pollution. For more information, visit *www.sandraingerman.com*

20. **Dr. William Tiller** is a scientist studying the phsychocnergetics of consciousness For more information, visit *www.tillerfoundation.com*

CHAPTER FIVE

HOME

*Now the real treasure is never far away; it is not to be sought
in any distant region; it lies in the innermost recess of our own
home, that is to say, our own heart, our innermost being.
But there is the odd and persistent fact that it is only after a faithful
journey to a distant region, a foreign country, a strange land,
that the meaning of the inner voice that is to guide our quest
may be revealed to us.*

—HEINRICH ZIMMER, *MYTHS AND SYMBOLS IN INDIAN ART
AND CIVILIZATION*

There is a little cove on the shore of Fernandina Island in the Galapagos archipelago where I once lived alone for a week. The huge volcano loomed behind me and the open ocean spread before me on my tiny beach. I wasn't exactly alone, of course, as I shared my cove with a colony of sea lions, flightless cormorants, tropical penguins and lava lizards, and every day, the sea was filled with diving blue-footed boobies, frigate birds, and gulls feeding in the waters.

The island, uninhabited by humans, is three boat-days away from the nearest settlement and is the wildest and newest, in terms of volcanic activity, of the islands. I was granted reluctant permission to camp there alone for a week, only because I was persistent, and because the director of the Darwin Research Station was a friend. For me, it was the dream of a lifetime to live alone on an uninhabited island. It was mostly for that I had come to the Galapagos.

Every morning I would rise with the sun along with all the other creatures, and eat hardtack and tinned sardines as the animals fed in the sea; every evening—the sun rises and sets quickly at the equator—I would feed on rice and spam as the seabirds dove in droves and the sea lions settled themselves and their pups in for the night. I settled in when they did, just above them at the top of the beach, crawling into my sleeping bag at dusk and lying awake for hours to gaze up at the Southern Hemisphere sky before my eyes finally closed.

For that week at the edge of the world, my little cove was "home." This bit of island coast became my neighborhood, totally familiar to me. I knew intimately the cove's pair of vermilion flycatchers; the habits of the lava lizards; the ways of the sea lions, their pups, and the noisy macho bull who ruled the colony, barking his way back and forth along the surfline. I knew where it was sharp and rocky underfoot and where the sandy beach started; I knew my way around the other side of the cape, too, where the lava bed rose into a tall seacliff. There I would sit by the hour watching for passing whales.

I had discovered where, just inland from my camp, there was a tidal pool in the rocks, and where a giant sea turtle had deposited her eggs on the full moon. At night, I listened for the hawk to fly over in search of prey, recognizing the sounds of his wingbeats. This remote place had become home.

It was endlessly fascinating, but after awhile I began to long for my own kind; by my last day there, I fidgeted nervously waiting for the fishing boat to come and pick me up. What had ever possessed me to travel to the edge of nowhere to be alone? I had begun talking to the sea lions and fussing around the cormorants' nests like a crazy lady. Sitting high on the seacliff that last day and watching a passing school of dolphins out beyond the breakers, I wistfully imagined my own house in Berkeley, with its garden and people passing by. There, I had a family who loved me and spoke my language. I could go to the movies and meet friends for lunch; I could call people on the phone, and walk to a market to buy tomatoes and carrots. Home looked remote and exotic from my present perspective—as exotic as the Galapagos had looked to me from the cozy familiarity of my home in Berkeley.

What is Home?

The word "home" derives from root words meaning variously "village," "family," "servants," and "dwelling." It is a place of residence, an originating place that a family unit comes from. I asked the scholar Clare Cooper-Marcus[1] for her definition of home, and Clare, who has written extensively about the deeper meanings of home in people's lives, had a lot more to say. To her, home is where we feel secure and in control of our environment; it is a place that holds our history and memories, where we put down roots and find refuge, the place where we express who we are and act out our personal dramas. Her book *House as a Mirror of Self* is about how our homes reflect who we are, and how we create them to mirror our deepest longings and our sense of belonging in the world.

I have known Clare for much of my adult life. Several years ago she invited me to go walking with her in England, on her native heath. As a child during the war, she was evacuated from London to the countryside, and her fondest memories of home are of the wild meadows, hedgerows, and farmland where she played and ran free with other children while the war raged elsewhere. A part of Clare I had never seen before came alive to me as we walked along the Cornwall coast, and she encountered the wildflower meadows, the English light, the complex smells of her childhood summers.

"See this?" she would say, picking a bright yellow buttercup and holding it beneath her chin, "when we were kids, if your chin got yellow, that meant you liked butter! Is my chin yellow now?" Nostalgically, she pointed out to me heartsease and speedwell, ragged robin and hedge parsley on the cliff-top meadows by the sea. Everyday, in late morning, we had to stop for tea-and-biscuit "elevenses"; afternoon tea, with muffins and cream, was a must. Only after several weeks of this annual infusion of "home" is Clare ready to come back to California, where she has raised her children and lived for almost 30 years.

The natural environment of the Adirondack Mountains, where I spent the happiest times of my childhood, holds a similar resonance for me. My body feels settled in that particular landscape of lakes and forested mountains, light and cloud formations, the smell of balsam and the springy duff underfoot. Although I have lived in California for most of my adult life, the gorgeous tawny hills and spreading oaks of our landscape, even the majestic redwoods and wild coast—much as I love them—still do not feel like home.

You Can Go Home Again

A few years ago, during a visit to New York, I set aside a day to visit the scenes of my childhood. I wished to revisit the houses I grew up in, my first elementary school, even the beach in Coney Island where John and I had argued in the winter storm. I hired Kenny, a friend of my mother-in law's who often drove her to her various appointments, to spend a whole day with me traipsing around the boroughs to seek out my old life. It was an unusual adventure for both of us, and we took off early one morning in his Oldsmobile for our pilgrimage.

On the road, we talked about the city we both had grown up in. His family had come from "down South," and my family had come from the Pale of Settlement, a Jewish Ghetto in Eastern Europe. I told him about growing up in our part of Brooklyn, and he told me about what it was like in Harlem before my time. In some neighborhoods he would drop me off to wander on my own, and in others he stuck close to my side, saying this was now dangerous territory. In the Bronx, he took me to the beach where he used to swim as a child, and I took him to the Beth Abraham Home For Incurables (now called something much more civilized) on Allerton Avenue, where my grandmother had spent more than 40 years of her life in a wooden wheelchair. We walked though the hospital very quietly.

Afterward, we ate hot pastrami sandwiches on rye and drank root beer sodas at what had been Weinstein's Delicatessen around the corner from the hospital, eating the same lunch I used to have there on Sundays after going to see my grandmother. While we ate I told him about her—how I had felt seeing her wasted life, week after week for years, until the day she died. He listened with glistening eyes. I loved him for that. In Brooklyn later that day, he discreetly stayed in the car while I roamed the halls and schoolyard of Public School 215, my mind a welter of memories.

I rang doorbells at every house in which I had once lived, and each time was met by terrified eyes on the other side of a door-chain and not allowed in. When I stepped into the dark alley alongside a childhood house on Billings Place in Brooklyn, where I had fallen off a sled and broken my two front teeth at the age of 10, the woman inside threatened to call the police. My growing-up years there had been fraught with sorrow, and I wondered if any molecules of my early fears still existed within the walls, contaminating the current occupants? At another house we had lived in when I was a teenager, I found myself standing right by the porch where my father had once slapped my face for playing checkers with a neighborhood boy. With a painful lump in my throat I said a small prayer for myself, for my innocent playmate Richard, and for my long-dead father. The memory hurt, but feeling the old betrayal and visualizing forgiveness, I felt a shift of energy as tears came—tears that had been held back all these years.

For the rest of the day, I repeated the exercise in various places I had once been humiliated: my high school auditorium; the steps of the Brooklyn public library, where a gang of girls had attacked me; the street corner in Manhattan where John and I had finally parted ways. I imagined the old sorrows, letting them dissolve and transform into a sweet neutrality. I cleared the air in places all over New York City—remembering, remembering. At the end of the day I was totally exhausted, but happy and ready for a good night's sleep and a return to the present. For both Kenny and me, the day had been memorable.

I wondered what my experience might have been like in a place I had been happier as a child. Would I find welcome there instead of suspicion? So a few months later, during a visit to New Jersey, my husband and I decided to search for my great-uncle Simon's old summer place in the country. Uncle Simon had owned a farmhouse there when I was small, and family members would vacation there in the summers. Mothers and cousins would go up for two-weeks, while the fathers worked in the city and came up by train on the weekends. The place was sold sometime after my 11th birthday, and I had not been back since.

It was so long ago, my only clue as to the farmhouse's location was that it was out-side a small town called Gillette. It was probably not more than a mile from the train depot, since I recalled that our fathers had always walked from the train when they arrived. Herb and I drove all around Gillette, but nothing looked familiar. We checked in at the town hall for possible ownership documents but had no luck. We then made one-mile forays from the depot in every direction, looking for a memory.

It took us two hours, but finally there it was on a tiny lane of a road, exactly as I remembered it. The once-ramshackle old farmhouse was now fixed up, the meadow alongside it still dotted with black-eyed susans and ragweed, and the woods I had never been allowed to enter just beyond. I even recognized how it smelled and what the air felt like at the end of the afternoon. My feet remembered the porch stairs. I knew where the old rocker had once stood to the right of the door and the muddy boots that had once littered the doorsill. This had been a place I had felt secure those few summers I had been here, and like Clare in the English countryside, its environ-ment was imprinted on my cells.

With trepidation we rang the doorbell, explained our mission to the surprised occupants, and were welcomed with open arms. They had never heard of my Uncle Simon, but they wanted to hear every one of my memories of the place. I started talk-ing and couldn't stop. Then they told of their extraordinary journey to this place—through war-torn Europe and refugee camps during World War Two—and I followed with stories of our summers here during that same war. Walking through the house, still so familiar after all those years, I pointed out where I had slept with my mother and sister; where the boys had slept together and flung feathers from all their pillows; how Uncle Simon had whopped them for it, but Aunt Jenny had later given them warm milk and cookies; and which window we had all stood at to welcome my cousin Teddy home from the war. Excitedly, I told them about the old kitchen furniture and the actual design of the original cracked linoleum, astonished at how many details had been stored all this time in my memory.

They were mesmerized, and we all sat at their kitchen table, our hands clasped together as we told our stories. We could have been family. It was an amazing day, and at last I mentioned the woods my mother had long ago forbidden me to enter.

"Why don't you go in now while it's still light," they suggested. "The path is easy to follow." Inside, the wood was indeed dark, which probably had frightened my mother. We followed the narrow path through the trees, presently finding ourselves on the bank of a gurgling stream—a stream I never had even known was there. Its water was dappled with late sunlight filtered by the trees overhanging its banks. How this stream would have entranced me as a child! I would have sat on its banks for hours, watching water tumble over those rocks and boulders. I had lost a lifetime of not remembering the delight that would have been mine on the other side of these forbidden woods. A mother's fear; an opportunity missed. I sank to the bank gazing, taking in the flowing waters, making up for lost time.

Home is Where the Heart is

I have had a recurrent dream since childhood that in my house I discover a room I didn't know was there. It is right off the kitchen, or behind the other bedrooms, or up a flight of stairs ... The room invariably holds meaningful treasures for me: a grand piano, gorgeous textiles, bookshelves filled with books I've always wanted to read. Once, I dreamed of opening a door to a cozy kitchen with bread and butter still on the table, as if someone—me?—had just got up and left the room.

Sometimes, in the dream, the rooms I discover are in someone else's house, but I remember them from when they were once mine; sometimes I find that my house has another entrance I did not know was there: when I enter I find a whole other life that I had forgotten was also mine. In each instance, once I've found these rooms, I can claim them as mine.

These dreams seem to be symbols for a part of myself that has newly opened up, as if my heart now has the courage to make a little more room for life to be lived. It is like recognizing that I do not need to confine myself to just one wing of the house but can live in the whole mansion!

The expression "Home is where the heart is" makes sense poetically, but it is also literally true. The heart is in the body, our first home. The "me" who writes these words, who feels these feelings, and in a little while will clean the kitchen and make supper, experiences my body as its dwelling place. We hang out together, my body and I, both when I'm awake and when I sleep. Its boundaries make it possible for my mind and spirit to move physically from place to place, to meet and greet my fellow humans, and to respond to my environment with pleasure or with pain. My senses experience the yellow fragrance of daffodils blooming right outside my window, and my blood will rise with rage if I am attacked. It is my task to protect my body when I have to—which I have not always done—and when the time comes, I will have to let my body die, perhaps even help it along, if necessary. There is a relationship between my "self" and my body, and I try to keep the lines of communication between them open as much as possible.

The body is like the smallest doll in a set of nesting Russian dolls. The next bigger doll is the house, the rooms, and structure we identify as "home." We "go home" to the place that, as the poet Robert Frost once said, "when you've got to go there, they've got to take you in"—the place where you "hang your hat." The neighborhood is the next bigger doll, and after that, the town. Bigger still is the bioregion—the natural environment of landforms and plants and animals. Bigger than that is our continent surrounded by its oceans. An even bigger doll is the planet, then the solar system, then the galaxy, and the billions and billions of galaxies that make up the Universe ...

Everywhere, in all these contexts, from the smallest to the most vast, we are at home. "I live here," we might say. "This is where I belong."

For the first 180,000 years of *homo sapiens'* existence on the planet we were all nomads, following game and the seasons. Now, only a few of us are nomadic. Home was the whole territory we hunted and made camp. Only after the advent of agriculture did we settle down in small tribal groups, usually near water, then identified that place as where we came from. It was also where our ancestors before us came from. In India, people still refer to the place they "belong to" as the place where their family has history.

"I belong to Kutch," my Indian friend Mhaduri once told me, even though I later learned that her family had not lived there in two generations. She identified as Kutchi, wearing her saris and combing her hair in a Kutchi fashion.

When I ask myself where I belong, I do not look back to where my ancestors originally came from. Their lives were too bitter; they were victims of persecution there and, indeed, never wanted to talk about it. I tend to look beyond them and identify as "home" the image of Earth as it is seen from space, suspended blue and glittering in the darkness, surrounded by mystery.

House, Home, Homestead

Very few of us have the good fortune to be able to design and build our own homes exactly where and how we wish, according to our lifestyles and individual quirks. Most of us rent, lease, or buy a dwelling that once was built to somebody else's specifications; we make it our own through the unique ways in which we utilize the space. If we own a house, we may refer to it as our "private property," based on British law of another century; in reality, though, we are temporarily borrowing a bit of earth with a structure upon it and calling it "home."

My husband Herb and I have lived in the house where we raised our children since we bought it in the 1960s. It's on a residential street in Berkeley, about a mile from the center of town—an old brown-shingle that was built in 1912 after the big San Francisco earthquake. My brother lives in a farmhouse on 80 acres of woods and meadows in rural Vermont, where he farms. He and 12 friends bought the homestead as Tenants in Common, meaning they co-own their property. My daughter lives and works as a musician in a small apartment in the suburbs of Boston. Each of us has had to make our dwellings our own—to decorate the four walls we find ourselves in to serve our lives, personalities, and needs.

I enjoy the process of turning an impersonal, empty space between four walls into a home. I could not imagine hiring an interior decorator to design my space, buy my furniture, or select the artwork for my walls. It would deprive me of the great pleasure of accumulating (and yes, overaccumulating) the things I want to live with.

As Clare Cooper-Marcus writes in her book:

> *We are all designers of the immediate milieu in which we live...*
> *We arrange and rearrange the near environment of our home, be it a room in*
> *a student dormitory or a house on its own lot. We feel nurtured by this place*
> *that seems to permit us to be ourselves, to relax into our innermost being...*

The French philosopher Blaise Pascal (1623–1662) thought that all the world's troubles stemmed from people being unable to sit still in their own rooms. Well, I can hear some people argue, "What if you don't have your own room to sit in?" And many of us do not, but we all have access to times of relaxing into our innermost beings, wherever we are. If "home" is not so much a place as a dynamic process, then every one of us is capable of consciously taking a few moments every night and morning, for example, to stop, breathe deeply and feel—right now. No thinking. Just Stop. Breathe. Feel. We can do this in the shower. Waiting in line. Riding the train. Make it conscious: Stop. Be there. Close your eyes. Inhale. Exhale. This moment is yours. Now.

Please do not try this while driving a car, however. After you have parked, two minutes will do the trick. The opportunities are there with even the most hectic of schedules, and if you can but be aware of them, you may use them well.

Right now, breathe ...

In-House Stories

Martin Prechtel,[2] the wonderful teacher and author whose imagination is boundless, claims that everyone ought to know the story of all the objects in his and her home. Where and from whom did this chair come? What is its history? What memories do we have of it? Who else has sat here? How might we glean its warmth and perspective from those who have come before us and be reminded that we will pass these things on in turn? Sitting here in my kitchen, on a maple spindle-back chair that came from my mother's kitchen, I glance around me:

The round oak table on which I write was once picked up for 10 dollars in a junk shop. There was a chip in the thick black paint covering it that revealed what appeared to be oak-grain underneath, so I dragged it home, and Herb and I spent weeks stripping and sanding the paint off, trying to keep crawling babies from putting the toxic stuff in their mouths. This cup from which I sip tea was brought back from Japan by our teenagers when they were exchange students there—the summer of my freedom when I took off for Seattle for a four-week dance workshop. The art photos of ripe tomatoes on the walls were taken by photographer Margaretta Mitchell[3] when both our children were small and we were thinking of collaborating on a children's book about vegetables. The silverware comes from our kitchen in India. This faded orange tablecloth was embroidered by Herb's mother when she was a girl in Germany. For years, I had seen it on her kitchen table.

When somebody I love leaves town or dies, I request some ordinary object of theirs as a keepsake and use it every day. My saltshaker belonged to a friend who died young of cancer; the small bowl for garlic was Jim's, who died of AIDS, and who I still miss daily. I think of him with every clove of garlic I use. Serving spoons and spatulas, teapots and kitchen strainers all have been bequeathed by one person or another through the years, and that way these people remain in my life. Our funny-face sugar bowl came from my sister's house and was made for her by our son Ethan when he was 10 years old. Over in the corner is her wicker chest. She bequeathed it to me on her deathbed, saying, "In the attic there is a wicker chest. It's yours. And everything inside it, too. But you've got to promise not to look inside until after I'm gone."

My sister was always playing games. So, in fact, I approached the wicker chest only after I had sorted and distributed most of the rest of her household. I did it ritually, my heart in my throat. There I uncovered a treasure chest of fabric—yards and yards of blue-and-white Dutch wax batiks, which for a quilter is nothing short of gold. I had never known she had it, nor what project of her own she might have been saving it for. I knelt there in her musty attic and sobbed.

There comes a time in your life when bringing more "stuff" into your house makes no sense. You are surrounded by decades of enthusiasms and gifts and the artwork of friends, and the place is overstocked. Karin McPhail, a longtime friend, once came in, took stock of all the candlesticks, photos, beautiful bowls, and vases on our mantelpiece, and said, "May I?" Deftly, she removed everything but one bowl and one photograph of a seagull stealing a penguin egg, taken by our daughter-in-law, centered them and said, "There! Now you can see them!"

She's right. So now I pass on certain treasures when the right person comes along to receive them. Those I choose to keep, I periodically move to different locations in the house. The rocking chair that has been in the guest bedroom for years now is center stage in the living-room; the quilt that has graced a bed for years is now hanging on a wall. That way, nothing goes invisible. It sometimes makes my husband wonder if he's seeing things when he comes home and stands in the middle of a room looking perplexed, knowing something is different but unable to figure out what in the world has changed.

The American Dream or the American Nightmare?

"McMansions," they are sometimes called, the humungous, overbuilt houses sprawled on an acre or more, often behind gates, in what were the woodlands and farmland outlying many of our cities. I have often wondered who might live in them, who would even want to? Recently, spending a week visiting friends in one, I discovered that not many people do. Our friends, a family from Crete here for a sabbatical, had been offered one of these houses for a year as a favor from the owner. It had been sitting empty for months, surrounded by other empty houses, their windows dark and sad.

Who were these mansions built for, I wonder? They are big enough to house families of 10 or more, but how many people have such large families nowadays? How much must it cost to heat all those rooms in the winter, how much time to clean four bathrooms? Whoever designed them didn't know much about kids, it seemed to me, and how many people know what to do with three living rooms anyway? Does anybody care that whole farm and woodland ecosystems have been destroyed for these developments?

As Clare might say, these places were designed as if the people living in them didn't matter. They are unaffordable status symbols that, given our strained economic times, were obsolete even before they were put up. I am reminded of the grand estates that Jane Austen's heroines aspired to, massive "castles" set in their own parks, miles from anybody else. Could you imagine yourself during a long, cold winter, more or less alone in one of those cold magnificences?

The sadness of those empty homes where my Cretan friends are living continues to haunt me, especially after riding the train through the East Coast inner-city corridor and passing through block after block of boarded-up, abandoned tenements. The neighborhoods there were dark and sad, piled with litter and empty of people. The train then passed through the suburbs, and again I saw house after empty house, plastic tricycles overturned in weedy yards, FORECLOSURE signs on the doors. Meanwhile, in the cities, growing numbers of people are abandoned, homeless, out on the streets, out of work with nowhere to go.

What is wrong with this picture? Something is gravely out of balance here, and we seem collectively helpless to change it. Why? I ask myself that question every day, suspecting some basic shared misunderstanding of what it means to be human in this world; what has ultimate value and what is secondary; what it means to live with respect for ourselves and each other; how to teach our children to share, think for themselves, and be kind to each other.

Ultimately, I wonder if it has to do with our inability to be profoundly happy.

Martin Shaw,[4] in *A Branch from the Lightning Tree,* urges us to live our lives with intoxication and ecstasy. He says that ecstasy is the key. I agree and wonder if the power of passionate feeling might be just the energy we need to take on the suffering in the world. If we lived in a state of courageous strength and commitment, we would not then turn away helplessly when a homeless woman came rattling down the street wheeling a grocery cart with all her belongings in it. It would hurt too much, and we would understand in our bones that her suffering was our own suffering, because we were, by definition, connected to her.

I expect that both suffering and happiness are really about our capacity to experience the deep joy of being at home together in the Universe—right now, right where we are, having this amazing gift of life. It is that simple, and that difficult.

Homelessness

I was in my late twenties before I experienced the problem of homelessness as a real possibility in my world. It was not yet common where I live in Berkeley, and the word hardly existed in my vocabulary. To say I was naive when we took off for India would be putting it mildly. So when, after a few weeks on the continent I happened on a bicycle accident at a crowded marketplace in the middle of Kanpur, close to where we lived, I did the unthinkable: I rushed into the fray to try and help. I was there as a medic, after all, and the hurt boy had been struck down. The least I could do was take his pulse and comfort him until a doctor arrived.

The boy was unconscious, and I shouted in my remedial Hindi to the crowd pressing in around us, "Where does he live?" We needed to get him home and into bed to wait for a doctor. The crowd shouted back, waving fists at me, everybody pointing in different directions. I had no idea what to do. Mr. Bajpai, my driver from the institute, shouldered through the crowd to rescue me, yelling at them, and pulling me out of the angry mob toward the waiting jeep. He was trembling when he got me inside and choked out that if that boy had died the mob would have killed me. What? Sadly, he explained that the boy had no home; there was no doctor. He probably was one of a million urchins living on the streets, grabbing what he could to survive.

That boy, who shortly sat up blinking and rubbing his head, certainly had not chosen to be homeless, nor have the thousands of people who sit on our own streets in all weathers begging for spare change. In India I was helpless to change things, but to my ongoing dismay I seem to be helpless here as well. There, I carried crackers and fruit with me and handed it out, mostly to children. At home I do the same; sometimes it is accepted, and sometimes it is not.

What do we do in the face of growing numbers of the poor and homeless? How then do we live? All I know right now is that there is one thing I can do every day, and that is to bring it all back home to myself, trying to focus on the joy deep within that encompasses both the beauty and the horror. When I can do that, staying as clear and hopeful and authentic as I can, I find I can be an effective agent for change in ways I had not predicted. Magic happens in small but potent ways. Sometimes it is little more than a shared smile; sometimes a real connection is made. At my food project, Daily Bread, some people get fed and other people get to help feed them, calming something in their own souls.

Even though none of us can change society on our own, nor protect all the souls out there who are in trouble, we can remember our own blessings and be grateful to those who show us so graphically that we are, indeed, blessed.

Homeless By Choice

I know a few young people, however, who have chosen not to have a home place at this time in their lives. Instead, they live everywhere, traveling the world to do their work. They think of themselves as "lightworkers," and they go from place to place teaching, working in clinics and gardens, volunteering in NGOs, and demonstrating healing techniques. Master gardener Doug Gosling is recently back from Namibia, where he travels to create gardens for orphans with AIDS, and he will return there soon. Healer Efren Solanas holds two-week healing courses back to back for much of the year, traveling from Brazil to Belgium and back again. Melissa Leo teaches English in Thailand, near the Burmese border. They enjoy their vagabonding life, and have fallen in love with the people they meet. I'll be interested to see where and when they land.

They are not alone in their desire to do their part in afflicted places of the world. Right now, I know people—not only young people—who are helping the recovery efforts in New Orleans and Haiti, teaching inner-city kids in Boston, cleaning beaches in Alaska, and holding camps for children in Bosnia. They are doing it for all of us, I think, so when a homeless person comes down one of our streets, we can remember that and not feel quite so helpless. The web is strong! May they thrive as they find the joy that comes from passionate commitment, and may they taste the distilled wine of life lived at its fullest.

Small is Beautiful

When we built the straw-bale cottage in the country, I learned that you have to know yourself pretty well to design a space from scratch that really fits your lifestyle, especially if there is more than one of you. How do you *really* live, honestly now? Probably not in three living rooms and four bathrooms.

When Herb and I gave it some thought, we realized that each of us spent most of our time at home in small, enclosed spaces with natural light. When I prepared food, I wanted a kitchen with stove and sink and preparation surfaces close to each other but with ample space around for people to gather and chat; and I wanted the refrigerator to be out of sight in a generous pantry. We both liked our bedroom cozy and contained, as we were there mostly only at night. But we wanted to have one uncluttered space in the center of the house—a main room, not necessarily very large—for spreading out.

Most of our time together, we both realized, takes place in the kitchen or the bedroom, but when visitors come, we tend to hang out in the main room. The result was a small cottage with one big, many-windowed room, and with thick walls of straw bales, each window enclosing a virtual alcove. A small sleeping loft above the room, a small bathroom, and a generous kitchen completed the cottage. The footprint was well under 800 square feet.

Colorful quilts were splashed all over the alcoves, where most reading, writing, and visiting took place, and except for the one with Herb's desk, the rest of the furniture consisted of portable futons and cushions that could be removed when we needed space for parties. It was small and elegantly rustic. It changed the building codes and started a trend.

One way of achieving this effect, short of designing a house from scratch, is to tear out walls in your own small house. Turning two small rooms into one large room suddenly makes the house much bigger and framing up a window or two to poke out a few feet transforms a small space into something magical.

Be careful, though! We once had a next-door neighbor who loved doing Sunday carpentry projects, often acting on sudden whims. More than once his wife returned home to find doors missing, or a wall torn out while she was away. His imagination was ingenious, and he created breakfast nooks and bedroom fireplaces, covered porches and hot tubs. But unfortunately, he tended to lose interest before each job was completed. You can imagine the result. His wife put up with it until, one day when she returned home from picking the baby up from childcare, she discovered the kitchen in ruins and her husband banging away at what had, only that morning, been the kitchen sink. We heard a terrible shriek coming from that house, and before the week was over she and the baby were gone. He never knew what hit him.

Small, portable shelters, have been designed for disaster areas, and could easily be used for the homeless people who find themselves out on the streets. House Arc,[5] designed by Bellomo Architects of Palo Alto, is shaped like a bean, made of light-weight materials, and can be shipped easily to places where it is needed. ShelterBox[6] is located in the United Kingdom and creates emergency boxes. Each box contains a tent that can house up to 10 people, along with the necessary supplies to maintain them for awhile. These boxes are sent in immediate response to disasters around the world.

Nomadic peoples have always had ways of constructing temporary shelters from the materials they find around them—or indeed, cart the pieces around with them, such as Mongolian yurts or Romany (Gypsy) caravans. Building materials are as varied as the landscape: mud, grass, reeds, straw, sod, branches, logs, stone, or any combination of the above. They have the advantage of biodegrading right back into the landscape within a season or two. Alan Weisman,[7] author of *The World Without Us,* claims that without constant upkeep and repair, the average house built today will last 50 years—100 years maximum. Just in case we thought our private property was permanently ours in any sense whatsoever, we might think again.

Community

When my brother Leon was a young hippie in the 1960s, he roamed the country with a guitar over his shoulder and a Conscientious Objector card to the Vietnam War in his pocket, looking for "home." He put up his tent in forests and hilltops, coastal beaches and hippie communes all around the country, searching for a rural place with woods, quiet people, and community. Eventually, as the war went on and on, he found what he was looking for in southern Vermont and settled down in a commune on a gorgeous piece of land overlooking the Connecticut River valley. People came and went, but he stayed on and when the land finally came up for sale, he, his partner Deb, and 12 others decided to pitch in, scraping together enough money to buy it outright. As he says:

> *We've been pretty lucky in that our group has stayed committed to the idea of community and shared responsibility—even for those who have moved away.*
>
> *Anyhow, the whole thing is still a work-in-progress, but it has been a work-in-progress for 25 years now so, all in all, it has helped make doable what otherwise would likely have not been doable ... It all boils down to how one chooses to spend their time. To do the homestead kind of thing, though, the first step is to get landed—and then the next step is to stay landed. Being connected to one's community—however this is defined—is of course central to making these two things happen. Can't do it by yo'self. So you got to work on making your community a happening thing. Time spent on this will pay huge dividends.*

"Can't do it by yo'self." Yup. Over the past 25 years, I've visited the farm in Vermont as often as I can. I go there for family visits and writing retreats, and one summer I got a job in the area for three months. It's my second home.

Every Sunday afternoon, rain or shine, people gather at the farm to play volleyball—inside the local school gym if it's pouring out. For more than 20 years, friends from all over New England know that if they show up at Red Clover on any Sunday, a volleyball game will be in progress at 5 p.m., and the players will gather for a potluck supper after that. In a world of accumulating complexity and change, this volleyball game has been like a steady heartbeat you can count on, no matter what. My brother and Deb, in their own quiet way, keep it like that. So simple, so good.

Their community, over time, has become an extension of my own community, so I've been around for a few of their crises. The beaver dam flood, for example. The rains had been hard that summer, the beavers had taken up residence in the brook, and a neighbor's fields and driveway were under three feet of water. One morning about 12 of us went over to pitch in with straw and sandbags, grappling hooks and knee-high boots, dismantling the dam and channeling the water away. It was hard work, but we had fun, and the grateful folks in the neighboring house had a pot of soup on for everyone when the job was finished. Of course, they would do the same for the rest of us, when (not *if*) the need arises.

In places where winters are as long and hard as they are in Vermont, the need for mutual self-help is a given. To get through the winter—especially if you are very young or very old—you need all the help you can get. This is understood, and people take care of each other. My brother has always brought in and split his own wood, and each year he does the same for the older woman next door. He and Deb plant an extra field of onions and butternut squash every summer and distribute burlap bags of them to elderly friends in the area, and the maple syrup they produce each year is everyone's favorite holiday present.

In this community, people share their lives—and their deaths. When a beloved woman in the community, living right up the road, was dying of cancer, everyone gathered round and took care of her at home. She had always wanted a screened-in porch, so a group of friends organized themselves and built one! I spent many an hour there with her, taking my turn at caregiving while I was visiting the farm, reminiscing, and learning from her how to make quilts. As I write these words, I am sitting warm beneath the blue-and-orange quilt she bequeathed to me, missing Snoo and remembering her with love.

In my experience, it often takes a crisis of some sort for people to pull together and realize, as my brother puts it, that "you can't do it by yo'self." When the Loma Prieta earthquake hit the San Francisco Bay Area everyone was out on the streets, helping turn off each other's water and gaslines and making sure the elders on the block were all right. Everyone knows it takes a village to bring in the hay, to raise a barn, to harvest the corn, to raise a child. But what if you live in the city in your own apartment; what if people don't know each other? What if you live in a place where the winters are *not* hard?

Well, for starters, you can get to know the neighbors by inviting them over for tea.

Neighbors

When our children were all in school and the district schoolteachers went out on strike at the beginning of one fall term, our family had a first-hand experience of the village rising up for everyone's benefit. The strike was a bitter one, and the battle lines were tightly drawn, so we knew this would not be settled quickly. What to do? All three of our children were in the public schools, so with a few other families on the block, we decided to put together a small neighborhood school until the strike was settled.

Since Herb teaches chemistry at the university, he offered to be the science teacher. Brenda, a nurse down the street, said she would teach anatomy when she wasn't at work. I would teach creative writing. Misha, the orchestra conductor around the corner, said he would lead a kids' chorus and, why not, an orchestra, too! Jackson, up the block, offered to write a play for the kids to perform if Elena would direct it. Our son Michael, who was a math whiz, would teach the little kids arithmetic. John, a few doors away, was an entomologist and offered to teach us all about bugs. Gus and Flora, the Lutheran pastor and his wife, would tell the old stories. Everyone's children would be the students. Within 24 hours, we had manifested a neighborhood school.

We were 10 families, with perhaps 20 children in all, and rich in skills and passions we had never thought to put together before. Classes got underway in each of our houses, we had field trips and rehearsals, and every Friday evening we all got together for a potluck and discussion of the next week's curriculum. The motley orchestra entertained, and we applauded our offspring (and ourselves) in the closest community any of us had ever been part of. We had the best time!

After four months, when the strike was finally over, we were bonded to each other for life, very sad to break up our new "family." But for years after that—until most of the kids had gone away to college, in fact—we all gathered every New Year's Eve and performed skits for each other, laughing until we ached. It has been years, but just last week one of those "children," who now lives in another state, visited us with his growing family.

"See this place?" announced Andrew to his four-year-old, planting himself in the hallway that had been our performance space for all those New Year's skits, "This is where Grandma and Grandpa and Uncle Tony and I used to play Shakespeare!" And then he mimed the death scene from Hamlet, and to our hilarity fell to the floor, re-creating for his wife and children that memorable 10-minute adaptation of Shakespeare we had all witnessed on a New Year's Eve more than 20 years ago.

Sarvodaya

In Sri Lanka, Rick Brook tells me, the people of a village—all generations—came together to build a three-kilometer road. He was there to participate in the Sarvodaya Movement[8] (*Sarvoydaya* is a word meaning "Awakening of All"), which is based on the very basic need to both give and receive, sharing labor that benefits everyone and, hopefully, the earth as well. He told me about the experience of hauling buckets of soil from hand to hand ("an eleven year old boy on my right; a sixty-five-year-old woman on my left"). In the course of three days, a road had been built. Everybody felt like they belonged to each other, and what had been a village torn apart by war began to reinstate itself as a community of people with power and with hope.

"So many people suffer from a sense of isolation," he said, "not only needing companionship in their lives but also needing to be needed. We all have something to offer, no matter how small, and if nobody wants it, then something in us grieves." He thinks that altruism actually helps the brain to perform well. That makes sense to me, as I always feel better when I am doing something basically helpful.

There is safety and security in a close-knit community of people who depend upon each other for survival, extended family, and companionship. In Ladakh, they say that you are in community when someone's good fortune brings strength to the others and someone's loss brings grief to all. There, the community includes not only the other people but also the land and the animals. And when a new house is built—which every child is taught how to do as part of his/her education—not only the people but also the spirits of the earth are consulted.

Designing as if Children Mattered

When I was growing up in Brooklyn, it was commonplace for the stickball game in the street, or roller skating, or hopscotch to be regularly interrupted by the cry "Car!" and all us kids would back off to the sidewalks until the car passed by. Later, as a young mother, I taught my own children to "look both ways before crossing the street" and insisted they hold my hand before stepping off the curb. The dangers of the outdoors were real. They had more to do with speeding cars than with predators on the prowl, and the potential danger struck fear in all parents' hearts. In fact, in our neighborhood just a year ago, a child was struck and killed by an errant SUV right by the school, and I continue to keep an eye out for the neighborhood kids on skateboards and scooters, even though mine are long grown.

Until I learned about cohousing communities[9] and pocket neighborhoods, I simply took it for granted that streets had to be placed in front of our houses. I bought into the assumption that it was the only way, and the easy passage of traffic took precedence over the needs of people, not only children and elders, but all the rest of us, too. Whatever were we thinking?

A cohousing community is collaboratively planned and owned housing, where green space and common facilities are in the center, surrounded by individual dwellings. Cars do not enter the central commons; instead, they park in specially designed lots on the outskirts, so that children can play in uninterrupted safety within sight of the houses, where several adults may be watching out for them. Pocket neighborhoods,[10] designed by Seattle architect Ross Chapin, are the same basic idea on a smaller scale. They are a neighborhood within a neighborhood, in which up to eight small homes are designed around a central garden and a common house, which residents may use to share tools and appliances and meals or have parties.

Collaborative housing is not a new idea; it is as old as the tribal village. With a little imagination and will, we can all do it right where we live. I don't believe we need to buy into a specially constructed "intentional community," especially as so many of them are prohibitively expensive. We can do it ourselves in a thousand ways: Community just means "people," and for most of us, people are all around us, wherever we are.

Unintentional Community

I remember once, in my Daily Bread days, giving out food bundles in a very poor section of town, in a church parking lot at the end of the Sunday service. I was working with women from the community who knew each other well, supported each other through all their toils and troubles, prayed together hard, and laughed at everything they could—at the men, most of all. Here we were, handing out bread and milk and beans to people coming out of church who needed these handouts badly, and the deacons, all men, were going crazy.

What sticks in my mind about that day, aside from the heartbreak I always felt doing this work, was that the deacons of the church had forbidden the food giveaway to take place on church property. Why? It had something to do with the dignity of the Sabbath. The women from the Oakland Food Pantry, a feisty bunch even when not provoked, basically told the men where to get off and set up tables in the parking lot, sassy as you please. It was a tense standoff when the parishioners began coming out, but these fierce *daikini* ladies held their ground, discreetly handing each parishioner a bag of groceries, along with hugs and sly glances at the deacons blowing steam in the doorways. And at the end, each unashamedly took a parcel of food for her own family as well.

I didn't want to leave—ever. They were my community, these women of my heart. Going back uptown that day, I recall shaking my head with wonderment at my longing to stay there, in a community broken by poverty, drugs, and racism; where people were hungry, and even the church would not help; where the men worried about impropriety, and it took a couple of gutsy ladies to cover the breach. However, Martha Paul and her cohorts at the East Oakland Food Pantry had something I yearned for: they belonged to each other through thick and thin. With the help of each other, they endured! May God keep them in His Light and shine blessings down upon them forever. Amen.

Temporary Community

During the last year of his life, Duncan Campbell, who died of AIDS in his 47th year, kept company with a group of friends and family who loved him dearly. We all pledged support for him and his partner, Conrad. In his case, I think we all wanted to spend as much time as possible in his brilliant presence, because the loss we were facing was incalculable. We helped in the house, kept him company, brought meals, were there for Conrad, and when Duncan finally became bedridden, we took turns sitting by his bedside.

During those months, the group of us were like extended family, knowing each other as intimately as siblings. We were aware of each others' lifestyles, preferences, quirks, and schedules, shared food and stories, cried together, and tried to understand this disease that was slowly taking away a man we all adored. Duncan had been one of my closest friends for more than a decade, and I was glad to meet some of the other people in his life who I had heard about but never known. Through knowing them, I was getting to know him more deeply, painfully aware that at the end we would all lose one of the best people we had ever crossed paths with. Every moment, therefore, was precious.

Over the years, this has happened to me many times, as I become part of a support group for a friend who is ill or dying. The group of us bonds deeply through the shared love for our friend. We become something of a single heart beating in several bodies, as we feel the mystery gradually approach the bedside where we are all on watch. We are a numinous community, understanding ineffable things that are not ordinarily available to any of us individually, and we bond through our shared experience of a transcendent reality. We see each other as if in the Light, especially as the patient comes to acceptance of his or her mortality, and we become, to each other, quite beautiful. Often the dying person recognizes this transformation, too, and tells us so. Together, we recognize love as the ultimate truth.

But although none of us ever forgets the experience, our community is as evanescent as a flitting moth because the day after the memorial we disband, go our separate ways, and may never cross paths again.

Intentional Community

Community, sad to say, does not always work. It is not necessarily easy to pull off. People you like perfectly well in any other setting may drive you crazy if you have to live with them, and especially if you have to make decisions together.

During a disaster—a flood or an earthquake, for example—most people will pull together no matter what; but if a group is trying to find consensus about whether to serve sweet desserts in the dining room, or how much space to give our family pets, then all bets are off. I know, because those very issues were actually disputed with passion in an intentional community to which Herb and I once tried to belong.

I will never forget the weeks we spent discussing whether people might swim without bathing suits at one curve of the river at specified times. It was the hullabaloo of the century as people took sides, every aspect of the issue was agonized over, insults flew about, and consensus was never reached. Over bathing suits!

The deeper implication, I think, was that none of us actually needed the others to survive. We could argue about flimflam because we were all well-fed and warm. In any case, heartsick and totally bored, Herb and I finally decided it wasn't worth the trouble and left the community—which dissolved shortly thereafter, anyhow. But we also left behind beautiful land in the country, a long-held dream of community, and the straw-bale cottage we had just poured our hearts, souls, and money into.

This may be what my brother meant by getting landed, and then *staying* landed.

Bringing It All Back Home

The Universe, I find, can be depended upon to punctuate my decisions with a practical joke, letting me know when I've chosen wisely, and when I've not. In this case, shortly after choosing to leave the intentional community and stay put at home, a major winter storm blew down the fences between our house in Berkeley and our two adjoining neighbors. We all had small yards, but when we stepped outside the morning after the storm, we discovered that we lived in a good-sized park that had been hidden in plain sight behind all our fences.

Like taking down walls between small rooms in the house and creating one large space, the fences coming down brought back the land, with its trees and shrubs, its pathways and flower beds. It was alive! We were all enchanted, and even though we had not known each other very well before that, we decided to risk it and together clear up the mess of the old fences, leave them down, build a little tool shed with the wooden slats—this, by our wild Sunday carpenter—and hang a swing from the apple tree for the small children. We created what Clare Marcus calls a "green playpen."

Our new little community comprised five adults, seven children, one dog, and four cats, and we were as random an assortment of personalities as any neighbors happening to live next door to one another might be. I won't pretend that it was all charm and delight, but it *was* charming and delightful enough of the time to make it worthwhile.

We did, indeed, make a vegetable garden together and chat in the mornings over coffee; birthday celebrations were often cookouts at the communal firepit, and the children grew up knowing each other well. We might never have deliberately chosen each other as intimate friends, but here we were, committing our lives to a shared enterprise simply because we were the ones who were there. After all, most family members do not get to choose each other either. And over time, we discovered that neighbors, whether they know it or not, *do* need each other to survive.

Our first task—and I would suggest this to any people considering taking down their fences—is to meet and discuss seriously what you each want from sharing space together and what you definitely do not want. It may take some trial and error to learn how you feel about private versus public space; when you would appreciate quiet, how often you want to hear about each other's days, how often you are willing to keep an eye on each other's children, and so on. Just as you have taken down a physical boundary, it is smart to know what each of your social and emotional boundaries are—a good exercise in any case. Regular get-togethers over supper or coffee to discuss personal preferences are essential, and growing clarity about needs and issues that come up must be communicated fairly quickly, if this is to work. The main trick is to get to know each other and know what you can reasonably expect from one another. The second trick is to be as reliable as possible, so that the others will be reliable, too.

There is a third trick, and that is to have a way to effectively mediate conflicts. I am told that when two people in a Ladakhi village disagree, a third person will automatically step in to listen to both parties and help settle the argument. It is taken for granted by everyone that peace is preferable to conflict, so grudges tend not to get carried over time. Among Australian Aborigines, the traditional way of settling an argument was to stand the two combatants facing one another but far enough apart that their spears could not touch. Each man was backed up by his team of supporters, and everyone was encouraged to yell their heads off and punch the air and stamp their feet and gnash their teeth—but never make actual contact. For as long as it took everyone to get whatever was bothering them out of their systems, they created a big din. Then, when they were worn out and their throats were hoarse, they all wiped their noses and walked back together for the big feast the others had prepared. I rather like that approach. But for the rest of us, I suggest we learn the rules of conflict resolution and start teaching them to our children in the sandbox.

In our shared backyard we had our personal difficulties, of course, but in the long run I believe the effort was well worth our trouble. Taking down fences, after all, is really just a metaphor for removing the barriers between each other, which deep down all of us are longing for because, ultimately, all of us are connected.

Over time, one marriage failed—the one in which the wife discovered the kitchen sink dismantled when she came home to cook dinner; one person became seriously ill; and all our children eventually grew up and left home. It was not easy to take on the burden of our sick friend during the worst of it, but we did it as a matter of course. By that time, I think we simply accepted that taking responsibility for each other under any conditions was a given, and that we could count on each other to do that when one of us was down.

Herb and I are the only ones of the original group still here, but our new neighbors on both sides have opted to keep the fences down. It is the next generation of extended family, and I attended a second round of home births in the same house next door where I witnessed that first baby born more than 20 years ago.

It's good. The apple tree is budding again, and the rosemary is an explosion of purple blossoms. In a few weeks, it will be time to put in the tomatoes and cucumbers for the summer, and I'm starting a pumpkin vine for the kids. I think my neighbor Kelly has gotten a musical DVD for this week. We take turns choosing musicals, which we love to watch together, then we spend the evening eating popcorn, singing along, and getting silly. The kids think we're weird, and they're probably right.

Close to Home

It may be just as well that we had to give up our country property, because it was almost a four-hour drive from home, and the irony of creating a huge carbon footprint in order to live a simple country life was not lost on us. We were *not* treading lightly on the land. In fact, although I grieved the loss of that beautiful land and cottage, the timing was right for us to take seriously our effect on the natural world and to commit to reducing our carbon footprints by staying home. I learned just yesterday a new name for this: Staycation. It was time to have my adventures right here, rather than long airplane and automobile rides away, and to focus on going deep, rather than going far.

In his Introduction to *The Circumference of Home: One Man's Yearlong Quest for a Radically Local Life*, Seattle author Kurt Hoelting[11] writes:

> *This much is clear to me. If I can't change my own life in response to the greatest challenge now facing our human family, who can? And if I won't make the effort to try, why should anyone else? So I've decided to start at home, and begin with myself. The question is no longer whether I must respond. The question is whether I can turn my response into an adventure.*

Me too. Herb and I have been fortunate enough to have traveled widely for years and to have worked within biking distance of home. Now that we are entering the quieter time of our lives, we're perfect candidates for the experiment of staying close to home. I call it the "Slow Down Movement," like the Slow Food and Slow Money movements. Caroline Casey says global warming should be called "Catastrophic Climate

Change" instead, to give it more bite—being a direct result of our collective use of fossil fuels. In that case, to paraphrase the ancient sage Hillel, I have to ask, "If not me, then who? If not now, then when?" I am aware that not everybody has the options I have, but all I can do is start right here at home with myself, start small, and try to understand how, person by person, we might make this work.

Our family has lived in the same house for decades, and I know the neighborhood well, but I wanted to explore it afresh and see it with new eyes, if possible. Slowing way down, spreading out and sinking deep, like water, I was curious to know whether I would get bored with the familiar scenes and feel like I was missing out on adventures elsewhere, or if I would discover new depths in old places?

And then one day it all came clear for me. I was walking the six blocks up to College Avenue from our house to buy a notepad. That was my only errand. A new book was beginning to take shape in my head—this book, in fact—and I was ready to start organizing my ideas in one place, rather than on random bits of paper. The day was misty, just the way I like it, and the air fragrant. I felt unrushed, so was aware of the subtle sensations in my body. I thought to stop at the greengrocer's for fennel, noticing I craved that taste, and reminded myself to get stamps at the post office. Some neighbor boys were practicing on their skateboards, and I stopped to ask them to show me their moves, which they happily did. I met some neighbors, exchanged gossip, and stooped to pet a cat.

Nothing special, except that it was. I felt a spreading sense of belonging right here where I lived, interested in my neighbors' news and glad to share my news with them, noticing the blooming rosebushes along the way, and the kids who were growing up. I felt happy. This simple walk to the stationery store was satisfying, like a ritual, and as essential to me as air.

Then came the choosing of the notebook. Spiral bound or sewn? French plaid or speckled black? My attention was as focused and single-pointed as a Zen master's. That's when I understood that simplicity and slowing down could be a vehicle for something much larger than it seemed, something rare and precious—something that, in the ordinary hustle and bustle of life, tends to get lost.

For his year of staying home, author Kurt Hoelting drew concentric circles from his home on a map. The first was two miles around, the second was five miles around, and the third was 20 miles around. He decided what was walkable, what was bikeable, and what could be reached by bus or train—and, in his case, kayak, living as he does on Puget Sound in Washington.

When I started my experiment I did something similar, but I computed it by time: I allowed myself to drive anywhere within a two-hour radius, but no farther, and that, not frequently. For everyday living, I would walk or bike, take the bus or Rapid Transit—or stay home.

The Eco-City Idea

Richard Register, the owner of the Vegetable Car I mentioned earlier, is one of those thinkers whose vision is way ahead of its time. His life has been devoted to the question of how to create walkable cities close to home,. He proposes that we reshape our cities, towns, and villages—even suburbs—to promote not only our own health but also the health of the natural systems we live in. He calls his places "Eco-Cities."[12] They are places where natural habitats would thread their way through our dwellings: we would all live close enough to our workplaces to walk or bike: public transport would be frequent and easy to access; and homes would be designed to take advantage of solar, wind, and water energy systems.

Most of us cannot fulfill the infrastructure of Richard's Ecocity vision in the places we live, but we probably can revise things here and there to make a dent. Taking down the fences is a start, bringing the land in closer and allowing the natural world to reassert itself a bit can help. Taking the bus instead of the car; growing a garden with neighbors; sharing tools, appliances, childcare. Ask yourself what you'd like, and then dream it up.

When a new baby has been born in our community, or someone is ill, the rest of us go into action. Herb and I have been the recipients of this more than once. One of us offers to organize the friends of the person in need, and each willing friend selects a day to be "on call." On that day he might provide food, run errands, do the laundry, or whatever else is needed. When all the days on the calendar have been filled, the new parents or patient's family are given the list (nowadays, it tends to be done online) and know who to expect, when. What is most sweet about this are, of course, the bits of intimate time you get to spend with your friends. You get to share your vulnerable times with each other, and your relationships are deepened by the encounters. And when it's the birth of a baby, you get to see this new life still fresh from the womb. It doesn't get better than that.

Rick Brooks, of the Dane County Timebank[13] organization in Madison, Wisconsin, claims that many of the services we need are easily provided by each other, rather than by city agencies.

"We all have needs in common," he says, "and if we come out of our shells and offer to give time to someone in the neighborhood when and how we can, and they do the same for us, then we get to know each other." The time you spend helping out is "banked," and when you need a hand, you can ask for it from someone else at the bank. It's fun, and you get to know your neighbors, says this distinguished man who has been known to dress up as a tall carrot for the local spring fair!

One of our neighbors throws an annual Boxing Day Party, to which we all bring our Christmas leftovers to share. The kids run wild from all that sugar, and the adults hang out and talk until all hours. Many claim it's a better party than the one the day before, on Christmas Day.

Bringing together elders and children is not a new idea: grandparents have been taking care of the babies since time immemorial. Every child needs a grandma and grandpa; every elder with an empty nest (and kids living on the other side of the country like us) needs nieces and nephews and grandchildren. Even when our own flesh and blood kin are elsewhere, others are often as nearby as next door. Every young parent would love an hour off now and again, while an auntie reads to the kids or an uncle takes them to the park. I keep a stash of children's books near the door to grab whenever the need arises.

I know several women in their eighties who make their way, by whatever means available, to their local playgrounds to sit in the sun and watch the children play. As Marcelia Yeh confessed to me one day in her 85th year, when I spotted her sitting in her wheelchair at the edge of the sandbox, "I got wheeled here in a stroller, too!"

There is an old frame story that can be found in many cultures of the world, in which the young person sets out from home to seek his or her fortune. After many adventures and tests and obstacles, older and wiser now, they come full circle back to home where, one day they discover that under the apple tree, or behind a loose brick on the hearth, or beneath the eaves of the roof there is hidden treasure. It was there to be found all along, even when they were out seeking it elsewhere. Perhaps, though, they had to search far and wide before they knew where to look.

For the treasure is always right where we are, just out of sight. Until now it may have been invisible to us. Now is the time to come back home, to find our innermost heart beating to the pulse of the world, and to sink deep into the Source for our answers to the hard questions our world is asking us to address. The Source is the hugeness from which we all come, the interpenetrating reality that contains all energy, all consciousness, all potential, and which is our ultimate Home. Everything we can think of—and much we cannot begin to imagine—is part of it, including politics, the economy, the environment, education, all the way to our dreams and hearts and souls. Every single tick of it is Home.

In the end, it is about coming back to love, delight, creation, shared laughter. Cosmic fun. Serious fun. It's all right here at home where, after all, the heart is.

Beauty before me
Beauty behind me
Beauty above me
Beauty below me.
I walk in beauty.
—NAVAJO CHANT
FIRST SONG OF DAWN BOY

ADDITIONAL INSPIRATIONS

The Charles Darwin Research Station (**CDRS**) on the Galapagos Islands is a biological research station operated by the Charles Darwin Foundation. In Puerto Ayora, Ecuadorian and foreign scientists research projects for conservation of the Galapagos terrestrial and marine ecosystems. For more information, visit *www.darwinfoundation.org*

ENDNOTES

1. **Clare Cooper-Marcus's** areas of special interest include medium-density housing, public housing modernization, public open-space design, children's environments, housing for the elderly, post-occupancy evaluation of designed settings, design guidelines, healing environments, and the psychological meaning of home and garden. She is the author of many books and articles, including the newly published memoir, *Iona Dreaming: The Healing Power of Place* (Nicolas Hays, Inc. 2010). For more information, visit *http://kitchentablesustainability. com/appreciating-a-mentor-clare-cooper-marcus/*

2. **Margaretta Mitchell** photographs people, gardens, interiors, and other subject matter on assignment and exhibits her fine art photography internationally. For more information, visit *www.margarettamitchell.com*

3. **Martin Shaw** is an award-winning Rites of Passage teacher, mythologist, and storyteller, and has facilitated wilderness initiatory process for a variety of participants, from at-risk youth to company directors. For more information, visit *www.stalkingtherebelsoul.com*

4. The **House Arc** is an affordable, modular, off-the-grid housing solution where the pieces are shipped (ideally, fabricated locally) to the site and erected by the user or community. The first House Arc prototype will be installed on the Big Island of Hawaii in 2010. For more information, visit *http://www.bikearc.com/ houseArc.html*

5. **ShelterBox** is an international disaster relief charity that delivers emergency shelter and dignity to people affected by disaster worldwide. For more information, visit *www.shelterboxusa.org*

6. **Alan Weisman** has written several books and won numerous international awards for his work in journalism and literature, including the critically acclaimed *The World Without Us* (St. Martins Press 2007), which describes a post-human scenario of the planet. Weisman is also an editor of radio documentaries for Homelands Productions, creating reports for National Public Radio. For more information, visit *www.world.com*

7. The **Sarvodaya Shramadana Movement** is the largest people's organization in Sri Lanka. *Sarvodaya* is Sanskrit for "Awakening of All," and *Shramadana* means "to donate effort." It began in one village and has grown to more than 15,000 villages. For more information, visit *www.sarvodaya.org*

8.   **The Cohousing Movement** originated in Denmark and is a type of collaborative housing in which a group of homeowners actively participate in the design and operation of their own neighborhoods. Private single family homes contain all the features of conventional homes, but residents also have access to extensive common facilities such as open space, courtyards, community gardens, a playground, and a common house with a large communal kitchen and dining room, lounge, and often classrooms, laundry room, and guest accommodations. For more information, visit *www.cohousing.org*

9.   **Ross Chapin Architects** is known for designing wonderfully scaled and richly detailed buildings and gardens. They strive to create places that nourish the individual, support positive family relationships, and foster a strong sense of community. Based on Whidbey Island in Washington's Puget Sound, the focus of their work since 1982 has been custom residential design and neighborhood development. For more information, visit *www.rosschapin.com*

10. **Kurt Hoelting** has worked as a clergyman, commercial fisherman in Alaska, a wilderness guide, and a meditation teacher, leading a migratory life with winters in Puget Sound and summers in Alaska. In 2008, Kurt made a commitment to go car-free and to spend the year within a 62 mile (100-km) radius of his home, as a personal response to the challenge of climate change. He spent the year exploring his home terrain on foot, by bicycle, and kayak. *The Circumference of Home: One Man's Yearlong Quest for a Radically Local Life* (Da Capo Press 2010) is his book about the year. For more information, visit *www.insidepassages.com*

11. **Ecocity Builders** is a nonprofit US-based organization dedicated to reshaping cities, towns, and villages for long-term health of human and natural systems. Their goals include returning healthy biodiversity to the heart of our cities, agriculture to gardens and the streets, and convenience and pleasure to walking, bicycling, and transit. For more information, visit *www.ecocitybuilders.org*

12. **Dane County Timebank** is a network of individuals and organizations in Dane County, Wisconsin, that are working to increase efficiency, opportunity, and resource sharing through mutually beneficial exchange, building community ties, and community self-sufficiency. For more information, visit *www.danecountytimebank.org*

ACKNOWLEDGMENTS

I have a penchant for play, and have long considered my life an opportunity for deep play and serious fun. Then one day in 1998, I heard the phrase "serious fun" used on the radio by Caroline Casey, a wise and witty visionary with a weekly interview program on KPFA, our local public radio station, called "The Visionary Activist Show" (www.coyotenetworknews). I had found someone who spoke my language!

Ever since then, every Thursday at 2 pm, I close the door, take out my current quilt-in-progress, turn on the radio, and listen. Caroline is like a recharging of my batteries and will forever be associated in my mind with radical color of more than one kind!

Through her I have gotten some of my more quirky leads for this book: playful wolves, the use of water words in banking, Rose George's book on excrement. Again and again, Caroline confirms my intuition that the playful approach to our problems is the way to go. She refers to this as a time of "dire beauty" and encourages us to "dream the world we want into being," to cultivate an attitude of "reverent ingenuity." She takes on the world poetically and with humor, and I am deeply grateful for her ingenious self. Thank you, Caroline!

To beloved and stalwart friends whose critical readings of the manuscript clarified, corrected, scolded, and laughed in the right places, thank you a million times. Without your input, this book would have been riddled with errors. This includes: Herb Strauss, Christina Bertea, Anne Hudes, John Hearst, Jean Hearst, Ervin Laszlo, Carita Laszlo, Priscilla Thomas, Sarah Minarik, Tom Weidlinger, Clare Cooper-Marcus, Rebecca Strauss, Sharon Strong, and Joan Levinson.

Christina Bertea, above all, was a teacher throughout this process, informing me on everything having to do with water, from graywater to pee-pee ponics, making sure I was accurate in all details.

Thank you, Ervin and Carita Laszlo for collaborating on writing and editing the foreword to this book. And to Kathia Laszlo, who made the connection.

To Sharon Strong (www.Beneaththemask.com), whose line drawings grace these pages: Thank you for your friendship all these years and for your shining brilliance.

Without my computer cohorts I might have broken down long ago. My husband Herb, with amazing patience, again and again has helped me over my laptop's glitches; and the lovely Sarah Minarik took all my scattered references and notes and organized them into a coherent collection of information. Thank you both!

Richard Cook, I do not know how I would have fared these many years without your independent bookstore, Sunrise, on my corner. Both you and the bookstore have been a treasure of books, information, and friendship ever since our first encounter at our local library way back in the 1970s. Remember?

To the Bioneers conference and community (*www.bioneers.org*), I bow with admiration and gratitude, for it was at my first conference that I recognized that other innovators were out there creating the forms for our changing world, helping me to know that the time would come when we would all be heard.

I am grateful to the volunteers and coordinators of Daily Bread over the years, whose faithful and enthusiastic stewardship of the project assured me that it would continue in good hands: Ellen Zucker, Carol Jenkins, Julianne Morris, Patrice Ignelzi, and Becky Mills.

It is an ongoing pleasure to work with the folks at Findhorn Press whose commitment to a vision of a better world never wavers. Thank you, Thierry Bogliolo, Carol Shaw, Gail Torr, Mieke Wik, Sabine Weeke, Cynthia Barralis, Damian Keenan and Nicky Leach.

And to all the friends and family listed below who have contributed their ideas, stories, and innovations, I bow with gratitude. It's been serious fun, hasn't it?

Abram Katz	*Mr & Mrs Woiznich
Britt Karhoff	Franco Tazzari
Caitlin Sislin	Leon Cooper & Deb Stetson
Zelig Golden	Enrique & Miki Sanchez
Kait Singley	Song Ping
Julie Wolk	*Chottey Lal
K.Ruby Blume	Ethan Stang
Leah Lamb	Ethan, Anne, Rob
Katrina Zabalney	& Elizabeth Strauss
Wendy Oser	Judi Petry
Julie Shearer;	Doug Gosling & Rachel Gardner
Mark Sommer & Maya Sommer;	Adrienne Robinson
Rebecca Strauss	Cristie Reich
Kelly, Todd, Tristan &	Aenea Keyes
Skye Lohman-Basen;	Georgianna Greenwood

Anne Hudes
Christina Bertea
Ken Smith
Jeanne Pimentel
Alex Nowik
Brook Jensen
Melissa Prager
Sharon Pavelda
Cynthia Winton-Henry
Aliki Zaimaki
Sharon Strong
Jerry Wennstrom

Adrienne Robinson
*Snoo Heslen
Martha Paul
Kenny,
Clare Cooper-Marcus,
*John Lowenthal,
Madhuri Deshpande,
Karin McPhail,
Mr. Bajpai,
Efren Solanas,
Melissa Leo,

THE NEIGHBORHOOD SCHOOL

Brenda Senturia, Michael Senturia
Ruth & Martha, *Jackson Burgess, Elena Burgess
Tony & Andrew, *John Chemsak,
*Gus and Flora Schultz
Locke, Tim & Bart; Gerda Cooper
Ian & Katya; Ginger & Tommy Alexander
Ian, Leslie & Megan; Herb & Carolyn Strauss
Michael,
Rebecca & Ethan.
Ashok Basu,
*Duncan Campbell,
Conrad Martel,
*Marcelia Yeh.
(* deceased)

Oh wondrous creatures,
by what strange miracle do you manage to hardly ever smile?
—*HAFIZ, THE SUFI POET*

FINDHORN PRESS

Life Changing Books

For a complete catalogue,
please contact:

Findhorn Press Ltd
117-121 High Street,
Forres IV36 1AB,
Scotland, UK

t +44 (0)1309 690582
f +44 (0)131 777 2711
e info@findhornpress.com

or consult our catalogue online
(with secure order facility) on
www.findhornpress.com

For information on the Findhorn Foundation:
www.findhorn.org